The Call to Heresy

The Call to Heresy

The Prophetic, Charismatic and Mystical in Christian Religion

Robert Van de Weyer

Lamp Press

Lamp Press
Marshall Morgan and Scott
34–42 Cleveland Street, London W1P 5FB, U.K.

British Library Cataloguing in Publication Data

Van de Weyer, Robert, *1950–*
    The call to heresy.
    1. Christian doctrineI.
    I. Title
    230

    ISBN 0-551-01906-9

Text set in Linotype Baskerville No. 2 by Photoprint, Torquay, Devon
Printed in Great Britain by Courier International Ltd, Tiptree, Essex

Contents

Introduction

Most Christians today are heretics. They hold beliefs and attitudes which are contrary to the orthodox doctrines hammered out in the early centuries of the Church. If they were presented with an unbiased account of the teachings of some of the great early heretics – such as Arius, Pelagius, Donatus and Origen – and then shown the teachings of their principal opponents, most people in the pew would prefer the heretics. I have performed this simple test on Christians of all kinds; and, if doctrines were chosen democratically, heresy would enjoy a landslide victory.

Those who reach a pew, however, are only a small minority of those who are deeply attracted to Christianity: there are millions of others who would love to be Christians, but for whom orthodoxy is the stumbling block. Indeed, for a number of years this was my own dilemma. I was in love with Jesus, but could make no sense of his being 'God Incarnate'. I wanted him to be simply a human being, who had learnt the path to perfect love, and could thus show me the way. Worse still, the idea that his death had 'redeemed' mankind from God's punishment seemed both incredible and repugnant: to me Jesus seemed to be offering us a free choice – to follow his path or to reject it. On those occasions when I encountered the Church, I found its strict hierarchy in stark contrast to the style of community portrayed in the New Testament. And the Christian literature to which I was most drawn was that of the great mystics – many of whom had been condemned by the Church authorities.

I was saved from this dilemma not by Christians, but by Hindus in India who had a deep regard for Christianity. They told me that I could simply follow Christ as my

1

'Guru', my teacher of truth, and that 'redemption' was only one metaphor among many in the Bible to describe the sense of freedom which God promises to us. They taught me too that Christ, and also Paul, were mystics who had penetrated the mysteries of the Godhead, and that it was precisely this mystical insight that made them worthy to be spiritual teachers. And in the Hindu Ashram, I experienced a pattern of community in which every member had a special ministry, just as in the churches founded by Paul. Thus, helped over the stumbling block of orthodoxy, I could give my life wholly to Jesus Christ. And since that time (some two decades ago) I have been Evangelical in my passion to share the joy of Christ with others, and Catholic in my devotion to the Sacraments and traditions of the Church.

Is heresy wrong? Should it be stamped out? The history of the early centuries of the Church is often presented as a quest for doctrinal truth. As Christians reflected on the life and teachings of their Lord, so divergent ideas and doctrines emerged and the Church was forced to choose between them. After prolonged, and often bitter debate, so the story goes, the champions of truth were victorious, while the pedlars of falsehood were outlawed as heretics. Thus, by the end of the fifth century, the great edifice of orthodoxy had been constructed, to stand proud and unshakeable until the end of time. On first reading, this is a comforting, even inspiring tale in which the Holy Spirit seems to have guided the hands of the Church fathers as they chiselled out the pillars of orthodox doctrine. And the moral of the story is that now, as then, heretical ideas are sternly to be cast aside – even if we do not actually burn the people who hold them.

Yet the same story can be told quite differently. In the early centuries many ideas and doctrines, later condemned as heretical, flourished and spread, enjoying wide support, and many of those who held these ideas were men and women of great holiness and sanctity, wholly devoted to Christ. By the middle of the third century, however, most

Introduction

of the bishops and clergy were looking forward to the time when Christianity would become the established religion of the Roman Empire; and early in the fourth century, when Constantine became Emperor, their ambition was realised. Hence doctrines and forms of Church government had to be imposed which were appropriate to such a role – and the free spirits of many of the holiest and most creative Christians had to be curbed. The edifice of orthodoxy was thus the teaching most appropriate to a Church which enjoyed a religious monopoly, and which could give unequivocal support to the secular authorities. And this edifice survived for over 1,000 years because, despite the rise and fall of nations and empires, Christianity continued to be the sole religion throughout most of Europe.

Now, however, the religious era inaugurated by Constantine is over. Since the eighteenth century growing numbers of intelligent and educated people have questioned and rejected the claims of orthodox Christianity; and by the nineteenth century the working classes were largely isolated from the Church. Moreover, other religions now jostle with Christianity for adherents, and people feel free to choose whichever creed or philosophy they wish. Few Christians see any prospect of ever regaining their former status, and many prefer the humbler position that Christianity now occupies, free from the trappings of worldly power. So, like our ancestors long ago in the second and third centuries, we can look afresh at the doctrines of our faith, without the pressure of being the established religion of a great empire. We can again be open to the perspectives and insights of the great heretics, asking anew whether they can help us to understand the mysteries of our faith – and, more importantly, enable us to share our faith more effectively with others. The word 'heresy' comes from the Greek 'haerens', meaning 'an act of free choice', and was used by St Paul in that sense (Acts 26: 5). Christianity now has a freedom it has not possessed for one and a half millennia.

Undoubtedly some of the movements which the Church

3

fathers condemned as heretical were evil, and their leaders were either mad or bad. But in this book I have chosen the four greatest heresies, each of which has born wonderfully good fruit, and whose leaders were people of exceptional vision and sanctity. Moreover, although condemned by councils of bishops, none of these four heresies ever died; on the contrary, in each period of Christianity they have resurfaced, usually amongst people who have been looking at the New Testament in order to rediscover for themselves the earliest teachings of the apostles. Thus each of these heresies is firmly rooted in Scripture. And today these heresies are again bubbling up amongst Christians, bringing fresh insight and vigour to the life of the Church.

The first heresy is that associated with Arius, often portrayed as the arch-heretic of all time. He despaired of arcane theological speculation about how Jesus of Nazareth could also have been God. He wanted to stress that Jesus was a full human being like us, who shared our temptations and sufferings, and who through the course of his life grew in divine love and knowledge. Thus Arius, like many people today, wanted to seize Christ back from the academic theologians, and place him firmly in our midst, as a close friend who accompanies us on a journey towards God.

The second is the 'British heresy', promulgated by Pelagius, the only major heretic to come from this remote corner of the Christian world. Pelagius is often presented as asserting man's free will, against Augustine's doctrine of 'predestination'. But his teaching went far beyond this, extending to the whole mission of the Church. He saw Christians as prophets, bearing witness to a way of life in which every aspect of human existence – economic and political, as well as spiritual and religious – is transformed by the love of God. Thus the task of the Church is not only to convert people to Christianity, but also to change moral attitudes in society as a whole.

The third concerns the nature of the Church itself. Most human organisations tend to become bureaucratic and

Introduction

heirarchical, stifling individual initiative and freedom; and the Church has been no exception. Moreover, the desire to be the spiritual counterpart of the imperial government strengthened the dominance of bishops and clergy. But, as St Paul taught so vigorously, every Christian is endowed with a priceless spiritual gift, and only if all are free to exercise their ministry can the Christian community flourish. North Africa was the home of the first charismatic movement, led by Donatus, who sought to restore the Pauline pattern of ministry – and who, not surprisingly, was branded a heretic by the hierarchy whose power he threatened.

Our final heresy calls into question the very nature of Christian doctrine itself: it is the heresy of mysticism. As soon as the theologians tried to distil Christian faith into a series of doctrinal formulae, there were those who protested that mere words could never embrace the truth – and that such formulae would be a barrier, preventing men from seeing the glorious beauty of God. Instead, they taught that faith is a journey, in which words can be used only as signposts pointing the way. At first sight such an idea seems quite harmless, but, as quickly became clear, it undermines the position of bishops and priests as the mediators of divine grace and truth. Mystical movements from the second century onwards have almost invariably been led by lay men and women, who taught that all who truly seek God can enter a direct, personal relationship with him. The greatest of the early mystical teachers was Origen of Alexandria – who was eventually ordained by a foreign bishop, only to be condemned by the bishops and clergy of his own diocese.

Each section of the book is devoted to one of these heresies: the first chapter of the section focuses on the early Church, and the second chapter follows the course of the heresy through history to the present day. But my purpose is not simply to expound history; rather I believe firmly that each of these four heresies is vital to the renewal of Christian life in our own time. I do not by any means accept every word the major heretics uttered, and I recognise that at times the heretical spirit has been profoundly dangerous. Moreover, the heretics have often disagreed amongst themselves: Pelagius was most rude about Arius, and Donatus had no time for the mystical speculations of Origen. Nonetheless, I hope to show that the four heresies are interwoven, and together form a most inspiring vision of Christian life and faith – a vision which we urgently need today.

Part 1
Arius

Jesus the Man

Who was Jesus?

The first Christians were filled with a desire to share their new faith with others. They wanted to tell everyone who would listen about Jesus Christ, his death and resurrection, and the good news he preached. Above all, they were so amazed at the joy Jesus had bought into their own lives that they felt impelled to proclaim it in every market square.

Yet, who was this person Jesus Christ, whose love could transform the lives of his followers? Was he just another wandering preacher who, like so many similar figures in first-century Palestine, had impressed the gullible and the vulnerable by his miracles? If so, Christianity would be just another Jewish sect that, after a few spectacular decades, would disappear into oblivion. Or was he someone special, even unique, whose message was directed to the entire human race?

This question lay behind the first rift – the first of many – which took place in the Christian Church, in about AD 50, less than two decades after Christ's death. Jesus's immediate followers who had known him during his earthly life, including Jesus's brother James and the apostle Peter, had established a flourishing community in Jerusalem which maintained the old Jewish customs. To them, Jesus was the Messiah, who would liberate the Jews; thus the Jerusalem church was a Jewish sect, competing with other groups who were equally convinced they knew the Messiah. Paul, by contrast, had never known Jesus personally and had for some years persecuted the Jerusalem church. But then, after receiving a spectacular vision of Christ, he had started preaching amongst the Gentiles. For Paul, Jesus was not merely some obscure Jew, of significance only to his own people, but was the universal saviour who would reconcile all mankind to God. The dispute came to a head over whether Gentile converts should be compelled to adopt Jewish practices, such as circumcision. An uneasy compromise was reached, requiring Gentiles only to obey Jewish sexual laws, and to abstain from food offered to idols. But at heart the issue was about the person of Christ, and his relationship both to God and to the world.

The question became even more urgent as Christianity encountered Greek thought, and was compelled to justify itself before the sophisticated philosophies of Plato, Socrates and the Stoics. For the early Christian apologists it was not Paul, but John, who provided the foundation for their theology. In the opening verses of his gospel, John had staked even bolder claims about Jesus than Paul had dared to make. Jesus Christ was the 'Word of God' (Logos) made flesh. The term 'Logos', meaning God's power in the world, was already current in Stoicism, and also in various Platonic schools of thought. John was thus asserting that God's power had taken human form in the person of Christ.

The concept of Logos solved two of the problems which plagued Christian thinkers. Firstly, it explained how God could be eternally changeless, and yet still active in human affairs. To many Greeks, the God of the Christians – especially as depicted in the Old Testament – was simply a supernatural force in the world, working on behalf of a particular people, and could thus not be the object of universal worship. The Christian apologists of the second century, such as Justin, replied that, just as the words that came out from the mind of man do not affect his inner being, so the creative power of God's Word does not alter the infinite and eternal nature of God himself.

The second problem solved by the Logos idea concerned

the position of those who would not have known the historical Jesus, and yet lived holy lives – like, for example, many of the early Greek philosophers. 'Christ', wrote Justin, 'is the Logos of whom every race of man are partakers; and those who, like Socrates, have lived in accordance with that Logos are Christians, even though they may have been regarded as atheists.' Thus paradoxically, while nowadays John's gospel is often quoted by those who assert that only Christians will be saved, the early Christian commentators drew exactly the opposite conclusion: that, since God's Word was present throughout creation and in every human soul, all those who lived in accordance with its promptings, whether or not they knew the historical Jesus, would be saved.

Yet, while Logos theology sufficed for the early rounds of Christianity's encounter with the Gentile world, by the beginning of the third century it was taking a severe pounding. It was partly that it failed to satisfy popular devotion: Logos was a scholar's term which could never express the passionate love which people felt for the person of Christ. But, worse still, on closer inspection it could not reconcile the Christian conviction that God is actively engaged with his people, with the Greek insistence that God is changeless. As the pagan opponents of Christianity, like Celsus, pointed out, either Logos is God, in which case he cannot be actively involved with the world, or Logos is not God, so the universal claim for Christianity collapses. This, in turn, led to an even thornier question. If, as Justin asserted, people could live godly and holy lives without any allegiance to the historical Jesus of Nazareth, why should Christianity aspire to be the universal religion for mankind? Since, by the third century, the Church already entertained ambitions of becoming the established religion of the Roman Empire, such an objection could not be ignored.

Hence the race was on to find a 'Christology' that would both satisfy the Greek intellectuals, and would express the universal claims of the Church. There quickly appeared two opposing tendencies. The first was to deny the divinity of Christ. Paul of Samosata, Bishop of Antioch in the mid-third century, accepted that Jesus was born of a virgin, that through God's power he was able to perform miracles, and that he rose from the dead; but none the less he was a man like other men. Paul of Samosata, and men like him, were seeking to make Christianity more credible, and hence were scaling down its claims; and, while miracles presented no intellectual problems at that time, the idea of God becoming man was a genuine puzzle which deterred many from accepting the Christian faith.

The second tendency was embodied by Sabellius, probably a Libyan by birth, who moved to Rome in about the year 215. Rome was then the scene of bitter theological conflict between those who believed that a single Godhead could contain distinct 'persons', namely Father, Son and Spirit, and the 'Monarchians' who argued that such a view amounted to a belief in three gods, and so was incompatible with the Christian faith. Sabellius became the leader of the Monarchians, arguing that God simply has three different ways of relating to mankind, as creator, redeemer and guide; but this implied no distinct persons within the Godhead himself. While this view was superficially attractive, and at one stage enjoyed the Pope's support, it came dangerously close to asserting that Jesus was not a human being at all, but God in the guise of a man; hence his suffering on the cross was merely an illusion.

The fever of theological debate was so high in the third and fourth centuries throughout the Mediterranian world, that it was said that one could scarcely buy a loaf of bread without the baker asking your views on the nature of Christ. At times it amounted to little more than an intellectual game of the kind that appealed to the classical mind. At other times, political rivalries attached themselves to theological arguments so that the thirst for truth became subservient to the lust for power. But none the less, the future of Christianity as a world religion depended, then as now, on the answer to the basic question: who was Jesus?

The Man who Suffered

The last and the greatest persecution which the early Church faced took place in the opening years of the fourth century, and thousands of bishops and priests were arrested and imprisoned. It was in a gaol in Alexandria that the lines were drawn in the greatest theological battle the Church has ever known; and when Christianity was at last declared the religion of the Roman Empire, under Constantine, the Church erupted in the most bitter conflict.

In Egypt, the clergy languishing in prison were divided on how the Church should treat apostates, who had denied their faith under trial. The Bishop of Alexandria, Peter, favoured a mild policy in which, after the persecution, apostates would be welcomed back into the fold after a period of fasting. The Bishop of Upper Egypt, Miletius, believed that they should be excommunicated. So severe was their quarrel that a curtain was hung across the cell, with the bishops and their followers on either side, refusing to speak to each other. Amongst Miletius's supporters was a young clergyman from Libya called Arius, who was renowned for his spiritual zeal and rigorous self-discipline. He rejoiced in the persecution of Christians, since it enabled them to share in the sufferings of Christ; and he regarded those who denied their faith as turning their back on the cross itself.

There was a temporary lull in the persecution during which the bishops and clergy were released, and Peter duly welcomed back the apostates. Arius mounted a campaign against him, gaining considerable support. But a year later the persecution was resumed, and Peter himself was martyred, demonstrating extraordinary courage during his trial and execution. Arius was so impressed that he changed sides; and, when the persecution finally ended, Arius backed the mild policy of Peter's successor, recognising that forgiveness towards the weak was a quality that Christ himself had shown on the cross. He soon gained a reputation in Alexandria as a fine preacher and theologian. But Miletius's followers regarded him as a traitor, and studied his every utterance in the hope of bringing him down on a charge of heresy – a hope that was to be realised with spectacular results.

As with most of those who were condemned as heretics, little survives of Arius's own writings, and so we must piece together his theology from what his opponents wrote about him and his followers. Nonetheless, a remarkably clear and coherent picture emerges. The heart of his faith is that the courageous obedience of Christ on the cross is the model which all men are called to follow. Arius's ideas were forged in the heat of persecution, and he could only make sense of his own suffering and that of his close friends by identifying it directly with Christ's passion. It follows from this – and here is the source of what came to be regarded as heresy – that Jesus Christ must have been a full flesh-and-blood human being like us, facing all the same temptations and confusions that we do. Thus in the garden of Gethsemane Jesus was seriously tempted to run away and escape his fate, and only a supreme act of courage enabled him to stay, aligning his own will with that of God – 'Not my will, but thine be done'. Likewise, during his earthly ministry he was at times tempted to give up in despair, and, like any human being, he must also have faced sexual temptation. For Arius, Jesus could at any moment have given way to temptation, and so God's purpose would have been thwarted; and it was only because 'he was tempted in every way that we are' that Jesus can reach out to us in love, and lift us up to his level.

All this was deeply shocking to Alexandrian Christians who preferred to emphasise the glory and kingship of Christ, and it is hardly surprising that Arius's opponents soon gained strong support. But worse was to come. As Arius developed his ideas, it seemed vital to portray Jesus as someone who grew in virtue, rather than was perfect from the first, since this enabled him to share in our moral and spiritual efforts. Thus the text in Luke's gospel describing Jesus's upbringing, that 'Jesus advanced in wisdom and in stature, and in favour with God and men' became crucial to Arius's theology. Jesus, to be fully human, must have had free will; thus his obedience to God was not that of a puppet obeying the master holding the strings, but of a mere weak and fallible human being struggling to discern and follow God's will. Thus, like any other human being, Jesus needed to learn how to perceive God's will, and to gain the spiritual maturity to obey him totally, to the extent of laying down his life. The crucifixion is thus not the pre-ordained outcome of Christ's earthly life, which he had no choice but to accept; rather, it is the climax of Jesus's own spiritual pilgrimage.

Arius was no mere speculator, conjuring a theological scheme out of his own head; on the contrary, as his opponents admitted, Arius stuck rigidly to the words of Scripture, interpreting them literally, and justifying all his assertions with reference to particular verses. Indeed, his literal, even simplistic, use of the Bible annoyed his Alexandrian enemies, who were prone to treat the Bible stories as allegories and myths. Arius's favourite text was the hymn in Paul's epistle to the Philippians, in which Paul wrote of Christ 'emptying himself and taking the form of a servant', and thus 'humbling himself and becoming obedient unto death'. It was because Jesus was like us in every way that he could save us, showing us the route we must all follow: by seeing the redemption of mankind embodied in the death and resurrection of Christ, we are shown the shape of our own redemption. This led Arius to regard the Sonship of Jesus not as something unique, but as the position to which we should all aspire: in Paul's words to the Galatians, we

shall become 'through faith God's sons in union with Christ
Jesus'.

On the face of it Arius's theology was close to that
of Paul of Samosata, who wanted to deny the divinity
of Christ. And certainly Arius was rigidly opposed to the
Sabellian view which saw the Son merely as a manifesta-
tion of God. But Arius's position was more subtle than
that of Paul of Samosata, because he took seriously the
opening verses of John's gospel which presented Christ
as the incarnation of the divine Logos. To this extent,
Jesus truly revealed the love and grace of God. But for
Arius, the logos was not God, or even an aspect of God,
but rather a power created by God to fulfil his earthly
purposes. Thus, by embracing the Logos within his own
soul, Jesus was in perfect union with God; and, if we live
in accordance with God's will, so the Logos is active within
our souls too.

It was at this point that Arius laid himself open to
attack. Logos theology already had a long history, and, even
if it failed to solve the central puzzles of faith, the majority
of theologians were in no doubt that the logos was divine.
Thus Arius had stepped beyond the bounds of orthodoxy,
and his opponents could now bring against him the charge
of heresy.

One Person, Two Natures

In AD 312 Constantine rode into Rome, and proclaimed
himself Emperor. During his previous battles he had been
accompanied by a bishop who prayed for military success;
and after his final victory he declared that his triumph was
due to Christ's intervention. Thus, while Constantine's
personal faith remained a confused amalgam of pagan
and Christian beliefs, Christianity now became the official
religion. Not only did persecution cease, but Constantine
looked to the Church to bind his disparate empire together.

To many, like the historian Eusebius, this seemed the fulfilment of three centuries of missionary endeavour, and was a just reward for the blood of the martyrs; and, since as far as they knew only the barbarians lived beyond the imperial boundaries, the whole civilised world now owed allegiance to Christ.

But far from setting aside their theological quarrels to bask in imperial approval, the clergy now argued more fiercely than ever. And as the Church grew in wealth and power under the Emperor's blessing, so each faction had a material, as well as a spiritual, incentive to have its opponents branded as heretics. To Constantine these ecclesiastical disputes were an intense irritation, jeopardising his dream of a peaceful, united Empire. He cared little about distinctions between truth and heresy, so long as the clergy would stop bickering. So he decided to hold a grand council of bishops from throughout the Empire, to resolve all outstanding differences; and in May 325, two hundred and thirty venerable gentlemen gathered in Nicaea to do theological battle.

They faced a long agenda of issues which were causing division, such as the date of Easter and the relative status of different dioceses. But, undoubtedly, the most important was the Arian dispute, which had now spread far beyond Alexandria, and was threatening to engulf the entire Eastern half of the Empire. Arius, however, faced defeat even before a word was spoken, since his opponents had successfully lobbied a majority of the bishops; and, when Arius did speak, many bishops put their hands over their ears, so as not to hear his blasphemies. But even if Arius stood condemned, there was a genuine dispute on the questions he had raised. Some bishops wished to stress the humanity of Christ, and were prepared to accept the Son as subordinate to the Father; while others insisted on the equality of the two, and were close to the Sabellian position that Father, Son and Spirit were merely manifestations of the single God. Constantine, who was presiding over the debate, rapidly wearied of these abstruse arguments, and in an inspired moment suggested a compromise formula, that the Son is 'consubstantial with the Father'. This satisfied no one, but was sufficiently vague not to contradict either side's views, and under pressure from the Emperor it was accepted – and has been part of the Christian creed ever since.

If Constantine thought this would be the end of the matter, however, he was proved sorely mistaken. The conflict over the person of Christ continued to rage for more than a century after Nicaea, and led to two permanent splits in the Church. As at Nicaea there were two main attitudes, and these became identified with two major cities, Alexandria and Antioch. Alexandria, despite being the city where Arius taught, was more fiercely hostile to his views, wishing to stress the divinity of Christ. Antioch, in contrast, was associated with those who stressed his humanity.

The Alexandrian school produced three major thinkers. The first was Athanasius, who in 328, at the age of only thirty, became Bishop of Alexandria, a post he held, with two periods of exile, for 45 years. He was a small, energetic man, totally incapable of compromise, and would hunt down his theological enemies until they had been excommunicated – or they themselves had found sufficient support to have him driven out of the land. To Athanasius, Arianism, and anything smelling remotely similar, was not simply a misinterpretation of the Christian Gospel: it was not Christianity at all. The Christian faith under Athanasius was embodied in the doctrine of the Trinity, that God is 'Father, Son and Holy Ghost'. This means that each person of the Trinity is fully and wholly divine, and worshippers can pray to each of them as God. If Christ was not divine, according to Athanasius, he could not have been our saviour, since only a divine man could enable us to become 'partakers of the divine nature'.

Apollinaris, Bishop of Laodicea, sought to take Athanasius's theology to its logical conclusion. If Christ was divine, he argued, then he could not have had a human soul: a human soul is inevitably unstable and fallible, and is thus wholly incompatible with the presence of the divine logos within Christ. So, uniquely in Christ, the human soul was replaced by the Logos. But this led to a further problem – how could the Logos be united with something as base and degrading as human flesh? To this, Apollinaris answered that, by its ultimate union with the Logos, the flesh of Christ became itself divine: thus word and flesh were one divine unity.

The most bombastic of the Alexandrians was Cyril, who became bishop of the city in 412. He was an eager heresy-hunter and also a notorious anti-Semite, even promoting a riot as part of his plan to rid Alexandria of Jews. In his quieter moments, he was a brilliant writer. Cyril was aware that Apollinaris, by virtue denying the humanity of Christ, had contradicted the old adage, which in various forms had been expressed by theologians since the second century: 'What is not assumed cannot be healed.' Hence Cyril needed to portray Christ as human, without in any way reducing his divinity. To this end he used a Platonic idea, that Christ was 'universal man': he was not a particular individual, subject to the limitations of an ordinary human being, but was the perfect universal man of which all other humans were partial copies. To our modern minds such a notion seems fanciful, but to someone like Cyril, steeped in the philosophy of Plato, the universal man seemed more real than any particular person.

On the side of Antioch there were two famous figures. The first and most attractive was a monk called Theodore. He was a pioneer of biblical studies, rejecting the elaborate allegorical interpretations so popular in his day, and preferring a historical and scientific approach to the text – thus anticipating modern methods of Bible study. His profound reading of the gospels convinced him that Jesus Christ was a full, rounded human being, as Arius had portrayed him, who faced temptation and suffered pain like anyone else. He was dissatisfied with the Nicaean formula of the Father and Son being 'consubstantial', as it seemed to deny the humanity of Jesus, making him remote from all our experience. He preferred instead the word used by the angels who declared to the shepherds the good news of Christ's birth: that Christ enjoyed a special 'favour' from God. This might seem to put Christ on the level of a saint or prophet, but Theodore asserted that this favour was total, so Christ lived in perfect union with God at every moment.

Theodore died a revered and beloved old man, his works read with the deepest respect. But his pupil Nestorius had all the stubborn belligerence of Cyril, his contemporary and deadly rival. Nestorius became Patriarch of Constantinople, the new capital of the Eastern empire founded by Constantine, and he was eager to assert the pre-eminence of his See, while Cyril regarded the ancient diocese of Alexandria as senior. Thus ecclesiastical politics overlay their bitter theological disputes. Nestorius created an immediate storm by trying to ban the popular title given to the Virgin Mary, 'Theotokos' – the 'Bearer of God'. To Nestorius, this was blasphemy, since Mary gave birth to the man Jesus, not to the divine Word. As soon as Cyril got wind of the row in Constantinople he wrote to Nestorius asking him to retract. Nestorius adamantly refused to do so. At heart, the two men were divided by the same issues which vexed the bishops of Nicaea a century earlier.

The fortunes of Alexandria and Antioch swung to and fro throughout the fourth and fifth centuries. Apollinaris was condemned at the Council of Constantinople in 381 – the Council which gave us in its final form the statement of Christian belief now wrongly known as the Nicene Creed. Nestorius was outmanoeuvred by Cyril and condemned at the Council of Ephesus in 431; and as a consequence a large number of churches supporting Nestorius in Asia Minor and Syria broke away, forming a new church which in due course spread eastwards into Russia, and even sent the first missionaries to China. But by 451 Western clergy had made common cause with those of Antioch, and at the Council of Chalcedon an awkward compromise was reached in which Jesus was declared 'truly God and truly man . . . with two natures, without confusion, without change, without division, without separation, the difference of the natures being by no means taken away by reason of their union.'

The formula of Chalcedon did not solve the problems with which theologians had been wrestling with such vigour, and raised new questions of its own. It encouraged people, if they read the gospels, to divide the words of Jesus into two categories, those which were human, and those which were divine. For the Alexandrians, in particular, it was unacceptable, and the Church in Egypt broke away, taking with it the newly established Ethiopian Church. But for the rest of the Christian world, it proved to be a workable, if rather crude, statement of a mystery which none could honestly fathom. By maintaining the divinity of Christ, and by asserting the uniqueness of the Incarnation, it upheld the exclusive claims of the Church as offering the only route to salvation; and thus it justified Christianity's place as the sole religion of the civilised world. And by acknowledging Christ's humanity, albeit in somewhat attenuated form, he remained a figure with which ordinary people could identify.

Model for Living

Anselm's Paradox

The doctrinal formula, hammered out at Chalcedon in
451, proved remarkably durable. Although it was an
awkward compromise between two contrary views, it was
soon accepted by the majority of Christians as expressing
the fundamental truth of their faith. And although its language is contorted and obscure, people were relieved that it
marked the close of centuries of theological wrangling.

The Chalcedon formula had two major advantages. The
first was that it satisfied popular piety. Ordinary members
of every faith wish to elevate their leaders to divine status,
and so make them objects of devotion. Within only a few
years of Christ's death, Christians had been making claims
for Jesus far beyond those he had made for himself, and by
the second century Jesus was being worshipped as divine.
Thus the Council of Chalcedon was simply giving official
blessing to popular practice. In the centuries that followed,
and especially in the medieval period, the most magnificent
works of art and architecture were fashioned to honour the
wandering preacher from Nazareth; and colourful, extrava-
gant festivals were celebrated in his name. Only a god could
have warranted such treatment.

But Chalcedon served another purpose that was even
more vital. By the third century many Christian leaders
were striving to make their faith the official religion of
the Empire, and the victory of Constantine in 312 marked
the fulfilment of these hopes. Thereafter the Church had
to frame its doctrines to justify its position as the sole
legitimate religious institution. If Jesus had been merely

a prophet – albeit a supremely holy one – he would have had no higher status than other holy men claiming divine inspiration, so Christianity could not assert itself as the only true faith. But if Jesus was divine, and more especially if he was the unique incarnation of God, then Christianity alone possessed the full truth. Thus the Chalcedon doctrine was the sword with which the Church held spiritual power. After the collapse of the western half of the Empire in 410, doctrinal claims became even more important in securing political patronage and support; and, for over a millennium, as empires and kingdoms rose and fell across the face of Europe, Christianity maintained its position as the sole religion.

Yet Chalcedon did not mark the end of intellectual activity within the Church. Theologians continued to discuss the ancient doctrinal formulae, and to seek new ways of expressing old truths. And although the incarnation was no longer the major sphere of debate, it still provoked awkward questions. The old Greek anxiety, that God could not become man and yet still remain infinite and eternal, was still a source of concern. But to this were added two further questions. Firstly, it was asked, how could the obedience of a single person – even if that person was divine – secure the obedience and salvation of millions of ordinary human beings? Secondly, even if the incarnation of his Son was the only way that God could save mankind, how could one be sure that Jesus of Nazareth, a carpenter's son in a remote corner of the Roman Empire, was himself the incarnate Son of God?

It was these questions which taxed the mind of one of the greatest of medieval thinkers, Anselm, a Benedictine abbot who became Archbishop of Canterbury. Anselm was born into an aristocratic family in the Piedmont region of north-west Italy, and was educated to pursue a political career. But in the face of bitter opposition from his family, he travelled to join the powerful Abbey of Bec in Normandy; and at the age of thirty became its abbot. At first he was caught up almost wholly in his administrative duties, but soon both monks and lay people came seeking his spiritual advice. The most common problem that was brought to him was dryness and boredom in prayer, so he began to write special meditations which people could use in their private devotions. The most powerful of these meditations are addressed to the person of Christ, whom he calls 'my beloved'. It is not so much a god to whom he is speaking, but a lover and a friend: he longed to be near Jesus, looking into his face, enjoying his conversation, and rejoicing in his beauty. He pours out his intense emotions to Jesus, asking him to respond with counsel and comfort. Other meditations are addressed to lesser figures in the gospels, such as Mary and Peter, and, as with Jesus, he loves them as close companions with whom he can share his feelings. To the people of his time, Anselm's prayers were bold and startling, partly because of their stark honesty, but also because he transformed the remote figures of the Bible, especially Jesus himself, into warm human beings.

In middle age Anselm turned his attention to questions of theology. He was anxious that much Christian doctrine seemed to rest on very flimsy historical and empirical foundations. It was not obvious to Anselm's eyes that the world was brought into existence by a benign Creator, since there was so much suffering and disorder. Thus the traditional argument for the existence of God, that the beauty and harmony of the universe could only have been created by an almighty divine being, was highly dubious. Equally, it was far from obvious, reading the Gospel accounts, that the historical person of Jesus of Nazareth was truly God incarnate. There is nothing in his words or behaviour that demands such an explanation, since all that he said and did could have been accomplished by any human being of great sanctity. Hence Anselm had to find another philosophical basis for the Christian faith.

He developed what has become known as the 'ontological' approach, which tries to prove the existence of God and the Incarnation without empirical evidence. Anselm defines God as 'a being than which none greater can be conceived', and he argues that it is logically necessary for such a being to exist. Every being in nature – every animal, every person, every idea – implies the existence of some being greater than itself; thus ultimately every being points to the existence of a Supreme Being, whom we call God. On the face of it, this will imply that God is remote from normal human experience, as, by definition, he is superior to any concepts and feelings we may have about him. But Anselm argues that the opposite is the case. If we rank the qualities of mankind from the lowest to the highest, this will point us towards the nature of God, since he is above the highest. Thus Anselm can say with confidence that God is loving, merciful, just and compassionate, since these are the highest attributes in mankind; the difference is that God possesses these attributes in their supreme form.

Turning to the Incarnation, Anselm begins by asserting that such a Supreme Being must want all mankind to be perfect, sharing his own qualities. It follows that sin is an affront to God, since it drags mankind downwards; and so mankind must be redeemed from it. How, Anselm asks, could this redemption be achieved? A mere human being could not accomplish it since he, along with the rest of mankind, would be marred by sin. Nor could God alone achieve it since by his nature he cannot share the temptations which lead mankind to sin, and therefore cannot release man from them. Hence only a being which is simultaneously both God and man could redeem mankind. Thus, Anselm concludes, the Incarnation must have occurred, even if its precise date and location could not be proved with certainty.

Anselm's theology seems to our eyes to conflict with his meditations: in prayer he can speak very directly to Jesus as his lover and friend, but in this theology the Incarnation is an abstract event whose connection with Jesus seems tenuous and even doubtful. In this Anselm was a man almost a millennium before his time. Since the early nineteenth century, and especially in our own century, Christianity has been trapped in the same paradox. On the one hand, modern spirituality is focused on the person of Jesus, not as a remote abstract figure, but as a man who was tempted and suffered like us. On the other hand, modern scholarship has shown us that we know horrifyingly little about the historical Jesus, so that attempts to prove from actual evidence that the wandering preacher from Nazareth was God incarnate are futile.

The Disappearing Christ

In 1882, a distinguished biblical scholar, Julius Wellhausen, wrote to the Prussian Minister of Education, resigning his post as Professor of Theology at Greifswald. In his letter he gave reasons for this painful decision:

> I became a theologian because I was interested in the academic study of the Bible. It then gradually dawned on me that a Professor of Theology also has the practical task of preparing students for ministry in the Protestant Church, and that I was not fit for this task. Despite every restraint on my part, I was making my pupils more unsuitable for it.

Wellhausen's dilemma is one that has confronted every teacher of theology since the mid-nineteenth century. On the one hand, the students, once they are ordained as ministers, must expound the gospels as accurate accounts of the life and sayings of Jesus. On the other hand, any serious academic study of the gospels reveals them to be complex mixtures of history, doctrine and speculation. In practice today most men and women training for ordination are exposed to modern biblical scholarship, and then, as soon as the Bishop's hands are laid upon their heads, their lecture notes are promptly forgotten, and they revert to a crude literalism.

The academic enterprise, which led to Wellhausens's resignation, had begun a century earlier with the highest hopes. A lecturer on Oriental languages in Hamburg, Hermann Samuel Reimarus, published a book in the eighteenth century in which he claimed to be able to distinguish the real life and teaching of Jesus from the false pictures painted by the Church. His rather simple efforts led to a rush of books in which scholars tried to construct, from the evidence of the gospels, the 'historical Jesus'. They were confident that this could be achieved, and they hoped to renew the Christian faith by uncovering the real intentions of its founder. The first phrase in this enterprise was mainly concerned with the supernatural and the miraculous elements in the gospels; and most writers, imbued with nineteenth-century rationalism, concluded that these were myths invented after Jesus's death, as a means of illustrating his teachings.

This led to the second phrase in which the emphasis shifted from the activities of Jesus to his psychology. It was felt that if his emotions and attitudes could be correctly analysed, and if the development of his ideas could be traced, then his true teaching and purpose could be discerned – and perhaps too the Incarnation itself could be demonstrated by showing Jesus' precise relationship with God. The portrait of Jesus that emerged from this approach, such as that contained in Renan's immensely popular *Life of Jesus*, is of a courageous and high-minded idealist, who gradually came to realise his own unique unity with God. Unfortunately, these attractive portraits were ripped to shreds by S. C. Baur, who compared closely the gospel of John with the three other gospels, to prove that John could not be relied on as historically accurate: John's gospel was written much later, and was mainly a theological reflection on the Christian faith, rather than a literal account of actual events and conversations. Since Renan and others had relied mainly on John both for their pyschological theories and for their chronology of Jesus's life, Baur's studies left their work in ruins. Although a few scholars like John Robinson have argued that John's gospel was written earlier than Baur suggested, almost all writers since Baur's time have agreed that it is theological, rather than historical, in intention.

During the twentieth century scholars like Bultmann have employed all the tools of literary and historical criticism to decide what bits, if any, of the gospel accounts can be salvaged as factually correct. Bultmann himself pioneered 'form criticism' in which each segment of the text is analysed to see if, within its present literary form, an earlier story or saying is embedded which may date back to Jesus himself. Bultmann's conclusion was that the New Testament, including the gospels, tell us almost nothing substantial about the person of Christ, and should be regarded as the 'kerygma' – the proclamation – of the early church. The main exceptions to this are the sayings of Jesus, especially those found in all three of the 'synoptic' gospels, which were written down and circulated almost immediately after Jesus's death, and so are probably authentic. Thus the New Testament tells us a great deal about what the first Christian communities believed; but as for Jesus himself, we are like figures in a crowd hearing him preach, yet only able to guess at the personality behind the words.

Faced with such ignorance about Jesus, there are only two ways to maintain the orthodoxy of Chalcedon – and both are fraught with difficulties. The first is simply to assert, as a matter of faith, that the Scriptures are infallible: that Christian faith consists not only in commitment to Jesus Christ as the Word of God incarnate, but also in acceptance of the New Testament as the Word in written form. This is not a new notion: Protestant reformers, such as Luther and Calvin, elevated the Scriptures to the status of objects of faith, and freely spoke of them as God's Word. And in the aftermath of the Great War, the Swiss theologian Karl Barth swept aside the anxieties of New Testament scholars, declaring that the Scriptures bear witness to the unique disclosure of God's Word in Jesus Christ, challenging us unequivocally to accept or reject him. Barth would have no truck with natural theology, which sought to discover signs of God in the natural order; nor would he participate in attempts to uncover the historical Jesus, since this is to reduce Scripture to the level of human literature. To him, Jesus Christ, as proclaimed in Scripture, is our sole source of knowledge of God, and God's spirit offers us the eyes of faith with which to see that truth. In varied, and sometimes modified forms, Barth's theology has underpinned the fundamentalist and evangelical movements within Christianity throughout this century.

The other approach is to return to Anselm, and seek philosophical proof of the Incarnation which does not depend on historical evidence. As long ago as the eighteenth century, the historian G. Lessing had spoken of the 'broad ugly ditch of history which I cannot jump across', and concluded that the 'accidental truths of history' could never be the basis of religious belief. And nineteenth-century scholarship has made that ditch so wide that Jesus is almost out of sight. Paul Tillich, a German philosopher whose opposition to Hitler forced him to emigrate to America, sought to make human experience the basis of faith in Christ. He declared that 'participation, not historical argument, guarantees the reality of the events upon which Christianity is based; it guarantees a personal life in which the New Being has conquered the old being.' In other words, we discover the truth of the Incarnation through our own experience of being transformed through Christ's grace and power, and hence brought into unity with him. Tillich admitted that it cannot be known for certain that the New Being – the Incarnation of God – is in fact Jesus of Nazareth; all that mattered to Tillich, as to Anselm, was that the Incarnation had somewhere occurred.

Although Barth and Tillich have attracted many supporters, their theologies avoid, rather than answer,

29

the questions raised by biblical criticism; and both in different ways are false to the actual experience of being Christian. The charge that has always been levelled at fundamentalism can equally be made of Barth – that he makes Scripture the primary object of faith, and only when we have accepted its infallibility can we encounter Christ. This position is akin to that of the Muslim who regards the words of the Koran as infallible, since they were directly transmitted from God through Mohammed. It is thus a perfectly plausible view which offers clarity and certainty to the individual believer. However, it is alien to the primitive Christian faith, and is a distortion of what most Christians believe. The first Christians gave their lives to an actual human being, not to words in a book; and, despite all problems of biblical scholarship, that strong, enigmatic figure from Nazareth still wins millions of converts each year. To be fair, Barth and his followers are wholly devoted to the person of Christ; the snag is that the infallibility of Scripture is a false bridge over the ugly ditch of history.

Tillich offers no bridge at all, but seeks to rise above the ditch on the cloud of philosophy. Yet on closer inspection his position is strangely similar to that of Barth. While Barth makes the words of Scripture into the test of faith, Tillich in effect elevates the formula of Chalcedon to the same high place. The venerable fathers of Chalcedon were theologians, working within the philosophical framework of Greek thought and sought to prove the Incarnation though abstract reasoning. Anselm and Tillich alike, within the philosophical framework of their time, tried to do the same. But even if this procedure were successful, it would leave the ordinary Christian cold. No one has ever dedicated his life to a doctrinal formula, and no Christian martyr has died for the sake of an abstract theology. The infallibility of Scripture and the infallibility of logic are equally false as objects of faith.

When the bishops met at Chalcedon they had no doubts that Christianity was the sole true religion. Despite the persistent divisions within Christendom, the whole civilised world affirmed the primacy of the Christian faith, and even many less civilised areas, such as the Celtic lands of Britain, were embracing the gospel. In the past two centuries, however, this secure monopoly has collapsed, and today Christians must rub shoulders with Hindus, Muslims, Buddhists, as well as atheists and agnostics, each seeking in their own way to discover the truth. Any Christian who makes close contact with the other world religions cannot help being impressed by the holiness and the insights of many of their great figures; and this in turn compels the Christian to look at his own beliefs in a new light. Of all the doctrines that make up Christian orthodoxy, the Incarnation appears the most questionable. Muslims, Hindus, and Buddhists would all affirm that Jesus Christ was a great religious and moral leader; and the more open-minded Hindus and Buddhists, far from seeking to convert the Christian, would urge him to remain loyal and true to his master. But any claim that Jesus was the unique revelation of divine truth, that he was the sole embodiment of God on earth, is offensive to other faiths; and the Christian must himself question the grounds on which he makes such a claim. Two centuries of biblical scholarship have made these grounds seem extremely shaky and uncertain.

Yet, through all this, Christian spirituality today is more devoted to the person of Christ, more closely identified with his sufferings, more sharply focused on the events of his life as described in the gospels, than ever before. If Anselm's prayers seemed bold and startling in their time, today they seem almost commonplace: Christian bookshelves are now filled with the most intimate meditations on the person of Jesus, in which every detail of his human life is submitted to loving scrutiny. Gone are the reverence and awe with which prayers and hymns used to address Christ; instead the worshipper speaks and sings in the most warm and friendly terms. Jesus is no longer some remote, mysterious figure whom only monks and nuns, shut off from the world, can seek to imitate; today every sincere Christian desires to imitate Christ in his daily life, and reads the gospels expecting to find guidance and inspiration. There has never been a time, since the early decades of the Church, when ordinary Christians have felt so close to their Lord, and have so freely enjoyed his company on the path of life, as they do in the late twentieth century.

Are we, then, schizophrenic in our faith? Is there an irreconcilable contradiction between biblical scholarship and living Christian faith? If the answer to these questions is 'Yes', then Christianity has become a dishonest faith and, though it may provide help and guidance to many people, it does so by deceit. But if we are to seek the answer 'No' – if we are to be honest in our faith – then we must be willing to reconstruct from the foundations the doctrinal framework within which we can love and follow Christ. Nine hundred years ago Anselm sought to defend Christian orthodoxy by means of a brilliant and subtle piece of philosophy; and in our time Tillich, and in a different way Barth, have sought to do the same. Yet in truth they have been defending the wrong position. Doctrinal formulae are not the objects of faith, but the man-made servants of faith, and if a particular formula becomes a stumbling block, it should be discarded. It is not orthodoxy, but living Christian faith, which needs to be upheld and strengthened, and we must fashion our doctrines to express honestly and coherently the faith which ordinary Christians possess.

Prophet, Pastor, Pilgrim

Ever since the Council of Chalcedon in AD 451, people have taken for granted that being a Christian involves believing that Jesus Christ was the Incarnation of God. In Christian countries children grew up to accept this as true; and, if in adult life, they experienced some intense spiritual experience, which they interpreted as 'conversion', it merely affirmed the doctrines they had inherited. Missionaries, who took the Gospel to other continents, likewise preached the Incarnation as an essential element of Christianity. And even though this proved a notorious stumbling block in Hindu and Muslim countries, the missionaries (with a few notable exceptions) never thought to ask whether the Gospel could be preached without the Chalcedonian formula.

But this was not the case in Arius's day, a century and a half before Chalcedon. Certainly many Christians did in some way believe that Jesus was God incarnate. But many had no such notion, and would even die for their faith believing that Jesus was simply a great and holy man. So many who heard Arius preach on the humanity of Christ had no sense that they were listening to vile heresy; and Arius himself regarded his theology as orthodox and highly traditional. The difference between the early fourth century and the mid-fifth century is that in the earlier period Christianity was still one religion competing amongst others, while by the time of Chalcedon it enjoyed a monopoly. Thus, in Arius's time, the Church was still preaching to people with no childhood knowledge of the faith; by the time of Chalcedon the vast bulk of the population acknowledged the Church as the sole repository of spiritual truth.

Today our situation is akin to that of the early fourth century. Now, as then, there are numerous people – probably the majority of the population – who have not learnt as children the tenets of Christian faith. Now, as then, Christianity jostles amongst a variety of other faiths and philosophies, and must therefore compete for adherents. And hence Christians today are compelled to ask afresh the question that taxed preachers and apologists throughout the early period of the Church: how can the Gospel be both attractive and plausible to people who are alien to the Christian tradition?

Anselm's prayers to Jesus were Arian in spirit; and so also is much of the spirituality of Christians today. Inevitably, if we are honest about ourselves in prayer, and if we identify our own joys and sufferings, hopes and anxieties, with those of Jesus, then it is to a human being that we are speaking. And it is the humanity of Jesus, with emotions and feelings exactly like our own, that Arius constantly emphasised. If we look closely at Arius's picture of Jesus, we find three key elements – elements which are present also in our own relationship with Jesus. The first is that Jesus speaks to us as individuals, calling each of us to repent of our sins, and to adopt a radically different way of life. The second is that he invites us into a community with him at the centre. The third is that he leads us on a pilgrimage, which he himself shares, in which we grow in wisdom, virtue and insight. The man Jesus who relates to us in these ways is not some fantasy, which modern biblical scholarship compels us to discard; on the contrary, biblical scholarship confirms all three elements in the picture. And such a picture is true to the experience of ordinary Christians down the centuries.

Jesus, speaking to us as individuals, is in biblical language a 'prophet'. He is, in clear stark terms, telling us how God wants us to live, and urging us to change our lives accordingly. Biblical scholarship has done nothing to reduce the impact of the prophetic Jesus, but has enhanced it. The scholars have agreed that the sayings of Jesus, which the Gospel writers have worked into their narratives, are from collections made very soon after Jesus's death. Just as the followers of the Old Testament prophets wrote down the major utterances of their masters, leaving us an authentic record of their teachings, so also did the disciples of Jesus. Thus Jesus preaches to us today as clearly as he did to the people who stood in a hot, sticky crowd 2,000 years ago in Palestine. Perhaps there is a small 'ugly ditch', because some of his metaphors and images relate more readily to peasant life than to our sophisticated urban existence. But, when Jesus tells us to 'love our enemies' and to 'forgive those who hate us', when he urges us to 'seek first the kingdom of God' and to 'have no thought for the morrow', it means precisely the same in the twentieth century as it did in the first.

The greatest service rendered by modern scholarship is to show that the New Testament is the product of a community – or rather a series of communities. The authors of the gospels and epistles did not sit alone in caves or huts, but were members of vibrant Christian churches, and their words reflect the living faith of the people with whom they lived and worshipped. The man to whom they bore witness had during his earthly life called together the first community of apostles; and soon after his death, the apostles became convinced that Jesus had risen, and was calling them to form a worldwide network of communities, which he would guide. Thus, if we for our part respond to the call of Jesus the prophet, then we too must become members of a Christian community of which Jesus is the pastor. And the New Testament provides us with the most vivid picture of such groups: men and women often fighting and arguing over status and power, people grumbling at their leaders, and the leaders bewailing the stubborness of their flocks. Yet their life together is infused with an invincible spirit of love, which heals their divisions and uplifts their worship. As we read the New Testament, and as we ourselves join a church, we have gone one stage further than the man in the crowd: he saw only Jesus the prophet speaking to a random collection of individuals; we experience Jesus as pastor, ministering to communities.

To Arius, a static Jesus, who was born perfect in every aspect and remained perfect throughout his life, had no appeal. If God is calling us to grow in holiness and virtue, struggling to overcome our faults and limitations, then Arius wanted Jesus as far as possible to share the task. And he found ample evidence in the gospels that Jesus 'advanced in wisdom and in stature' as he prepared for his earthly ministry. Jesus is thus not only a prophet and pastor, but a pilgrim also, walking beside us on our spiritual journey. Again biblical scholarship affirms, not denies, such a view.

Certainly there are stories in the Bible, such as the virgin birth, which may seem to assert the moral perfection of Christ from the very moment of conception. And some have argued that only a divine human being could have risen from the dead. But the Bible gives little support for such interpretations; on the contrary, the promise of Christ's resurrection is that all of us, at the end of our pilgrimage, will share his risen life. When with Bultmann we try to strip away the 'myths' that encrust the story of Christ, we are left with a human being on fire with the love of God, who is willing to follow God wherever he might lead, and that is the path which we too are called to tread.

Where then does this leave the orthodoxy of Chalcedon? Is the doctrine of incarnation now redundant, to be discarded after so many centuries? This is what, in 1977, was urged by the authors of *The Myth of God Incarnate*. To them the doctrine is now a stumbling block both to honest faith and to good relations with other religions. They argue that Jesus was 'intensely, totally, and overwhelmingly conscious of the reality of God', but that, in the words of John Hick, 'later conceptions of him as God incarnate, the Second Person of the Holy Trinity living a human life, is a mythological or poetic way of expressing his significance for us'. But, as Dennis Nineham asked in a famous epilogue to the book, how can we know that the man Jesus had all the outstanding moral qualities which Hick and others attributed to him? If biblical scholarship has undermined the old orthodoxy of Jesus as God incarnate, it will also destroy a new doctrine of Jesus as perfect man.

The describing of Jesus as prophet, pastor, and pilgrim is first and foremost a challenge to us today, and makes only the lightest historical claims. If Jesus is to be a prophet, only his sayings need passing on to us; what matters is whether we obey his commands. If Jesus is to be our pastor, we need as our source book the New Testament to show how the first Christians responded to his ministry; what matters is whether we in our communities can emulate their example.

And if Jesus is beside us on our pilgrimage, we need only know that he had to struggle with temptation and suffering, as we do now. Yet, paradoxically, by accepting without demur the ditch of history, and by putting the stress on present experience, the doctrine of incarnation begins again to make sense: the teachings of Arius point, is an unexpected way, beyond Chalcedon to Anselm.

For Anselm, the Incarnation was not a historical event, but a metaphysical reality, and, as such, the evidence for it lay not in historical research, but in the experience of men and women in their relationship with God. People can, Anselm asserted, experience unity with God, so the gulf between God and man has manifestly been bridged. From all that we know, Jesus crossed that bridge, and we as his disciples follow him. Yet there may also be others crossing that bridge, led by other prophets, pastors and pilgrims, and as we get to know people of other faiths more closely, we recognise them as fellow-travellers. The Incarnation is thus not some assertion about an event in history, which can be endlessly disputed by scholars, but a statement about spiritual experience, in which every human being can share.

In the following chapters we shall look in more depth at Jesus as prophet, pastor and pilgrim, helped by the thoughts of other great heretics. Sadly, after his condemnation, Arius was shunned by orthodox and heretics alike, and his ideas were grossly misrepresented. Yet the other great heresies that we are to explore may all be regarded as a single movement which arises from the desire of ordinary Christians for a warm, personal relationship with Jesus.

Part 2
Pelagius

Jesus the Prophet

A Good People

To the modern reader, the New Testament seems full of moral commandments. We speak of a 'Christian way of life', by which we mean a pattern of life in accordance with the ethics of Jesus; and the first three gospels in particular are stuffed with sayings on every aspect of human behaviour. Admittedly there are some discrepancies between what people assume Jesus said, and what he actually taught. It is often imagined that Christian morality boils down to little more than honesty and fairness in one's dealings with others, plus a charitable attitude to one's neighbours. In fact the way of life Christ enjoins is far more radical, requiring the disciple constantly to forgive others and to love his enemies, and to regard all his talents and material resources as belonging to God, to be used in his service.

To a quite remarkable extent the Christians of the first three centuries lived up to these high ideals; and this was the major reason for their extraordinary success in gaining converts. Members of the first church in Jerusalem shared all their goods, distributing to each according to their need, and met regularly to eat and pray together. And, as Luke records, their numbers expanded rapidly, with people being added daily to the group. While this experiment in communal living was shortlived, the Christian churches which sprung up throughout the Roman Empire quickly gained a reputation for their charity and mutual support. A Christian who fell on hard times was helped by his fellows, and the friendships between Christians were warm and generous. Christian families became renowned for their stability and closeness, with women enjoying a far higher status than was common in society as a whole. And in matters of business, a Christian could be relied upon never to cheat or deceive, and always to keep his word. In a society as sophisticated and cultured as that of ancient Rome, Christianity seemed crude and simple, lacking the intellectual verve or the lavish rituals of most of the other religious sects. But its high moral standards made it attractive to people from every class of society.

Yet, during this period, Christian theologians and apologists paid almost no attention to ethical questions: the nature of Jesus Christ and the basic doctrines of the church occupied their attention, to the virtual exclusion of matters of morality and personal behaviour. There was some discussion about the nature of sin. Justin in the second century regarded sin largely as a form of ignorance, due to the machinations of the devil, which prevented people from distinguishing right from wrong. Tertullian, the North African polemicist, was the first major writer to propound the notion of original sin, whereby evil is seen as inherent in the human soul, so that even little children should be regarded as morally unclean; but he also asserted that there was an equal measure of intrinsic goodness in the soul, and that through the exercise of his will the individual could cause the goodness within him to triumph over evil. A century later, by contrast, the theologians of Antioch, such as Theodore, were roundly denying the doctrine of original sin, ridiculing the idea that Adam's sin was passed from one generation to the next. But these issues, vital though they became to Christians from the fourth century onwards, caused barely a ripple in earlier times.

To an extent that is hard to exaggerate, Christian theology in the early centuries adopted Greek patterns of thought; and even today Christians rely far more heavily on ancient Greek philosophy than they would care to admit. In the matter of ethics, the early Christians took almost without question the ideas of the Stoics, and only by understanding the Stoic philosophy can we grasp the conflicts that soon were to engulf the Christian world, and that have caused controversy ever since. The Stoic school originated with the philosopher Zeno in the fourth century BC and derived its name from the painted colonnade known as the 'Stoa' in the Athens market-place where Zeno used to teach. The Stoics first coined the term 'Logos' to describe the power of God in every object: the Logos in their eyes was the essential quality of an object, such as the hardness of a stone or the sheen on silver. They also spoke of 'pneuma' as the motion and energy of an object. Applied to man, the Logos is his rational intelligence, and the pneuma is his will.

The purpose of human life, according to the Stoics, is to achieve perfect wisdom. This means that a person's Logos should be in complete accord with the Logos throughout all creation; and hence his pneuma, and his moral actions, will operate in perfect harmony with the movements of the whole of nature. Thus the truly wise man should never cause injury to others, because that would upset the natural harmony of creation. But equally, the wise man can never be injured by others, however much they try to hurt him: his Logos will be in such close accord with the divine Logos that no amount of physical damage, or even psychological torment, can destroy his interior peace. This led to an indifference towards normal worldly concerns, such as wealth, status and even good health, but equally it gave the Stoics very high moral standards, since all their external actions should be 'in accordance with nature', causing suffering to no one and promoting the harmony of all.

The Stoics also developed a subtle doctrine of fate and free will. They distinguished between 'principal' and 'initiating' causes of events: thus, if a ball rolls down a hill, the principal cause is the ball's roundness, while the initiating cause is the push that sets it in motion. Principal causes, or potentialities, are built into nature itself, and the pattern of events must always be in accordance with them. So, to this extent, we can speak of our fate as predetermined by nature itself –

and hence by God. Initiating causes, by contrast, are not predetermined by nature but are the result of human will; hence, within the framework of principle causes – which we today might call the 'laws of nature' – men could determine the outcome of events for good or evil. The Stoic philosopher Chrysippus compared man to a dog tied behind a cart, which he must follow reluctantly or willingly: the wise man follows the laws of nature willingly, and so promotes harmony, while the foolish man tries to resist nature, and so causes discord.

It is easy to see the attraction of Stoic philosophy to the early Christians. John's gospel had already used the concept of logos to describe the divine power present in Christ, and the word pneuma had been adopted to refer to the Spirit. So, latent within Stoic thought was a picture of God's relationship with mankind that was remarkably similar to that contained within the New Testament. Moreover, the man of perfect wisdom portrayed by the Stoics was remarkably similar to Christ, and the high moral standards which flowed from Stoic wisdom were uncannily similar to the moral teachings of the Sermon on the Mount. And, to crown it all, the Stoic had a most attractive solution to the puzzle of how the all-seeing, all-powerful God preached by Christ could be reconciled with the moral freedom of the individual: man exercises his freedom within the laws of God, which are embodied in creation itself.

But when in the fourth century an austere and devout spiritual counsellor called Pelagius translated Stoic ideas into a purely Christian form, and when these ideas were used by monks to denounce the growing wealth and power of the Church, a theological explosion occurred which has echoed down the centuries.

The Call of the Desert

Early in the fourth century growing numbers of men in

Egypt and Syria were leaving the comfortable cities, and wandering off into the desert to live as monks, devoting themselves wholly to prayer. The movement began during the final persecution of the Emperor Diocletian, when the desert offered an escape from imprisonment and torture. But it gathered pace after Constantine authorised Christianity as the imperial religion. The Church grew rapidly in worldly power and wealth, tempting bishops and priests to ignore their spiritual duties in favour of material advancement. Many devout Christians were appalled at this corruption, and sought in the desert the simplicity and poverty of Christ himself. Soon these monks were forming communities, and by the end of the fourth century the deserts of the eastern Mediterranean were peppered with monastic settlements, some with thousands of members.

In western Europe monasticism was slower to develop, but by the late fourth century it was fashionable for upper-class women in the cities, as their youthful beauty faded, to adopt an ascetic way of life, under the guidance of a spiritual adviser. Some time in the 380s Pelagius travelled from his native Britain to Rome, and was appointed adviser to one of the most powerful families in the city, the Anicii. Pelagius quickly gained a reputation for his clear teaching and high moral ideas, and soon had a following throughout the city. As one disciple wrote: 'I used to regard myself as a worshipper of God; but now for the first time I know how to become a true Christian.' To Pelagius, every Christian was called to live as a monk within their own home; and in the final decadent years of the Roman Empire, many sincere Christians found the idea attractive.

The central tenet of Pelagius's teaching was the moral and spiritual freedom of the individual. He believed that God, through the laws of nature and through the teachings of Christ, had revealed what is right and wrong; and each individual is free to choose whether to obey God, or to reject him. He combined this doctrine with a stern belief in divine judgement: the righteous person will receive an eternal reward, while the unrighteous will suffer everlasting damnation. He rejected entirely the notion of original sin: 'If in the womb of their mothers men were filled with bygone sins, it would make the Devil himself the maker of men.' On the contrary, he believed that each person is responsible before God for their own actions, and thence for their own final destiny.

This does not mean, however, that God refuses to help us with his grace and strength. Pelagius developed theories of human psychology and also of fate that were closely akin to those of the Stoics, and through these theories he sought to show how divine grace operates. Just as the Stoics distinguished logos and pneuma within the human soul, so Pelagius saw the soul as divided between power (posse) and will (velle). Man's will is always free, and the way in which we direct our wills determines the outcome of events. Our inward power, however, is constantly open to the flow of divine grace. If, as an act of will, we open ourselves to God, he will always give us the power to obey him and to resist temptation. These faculties of power and will are latent in all creation, and the interaction between them determines the course of history. The inward power of the human being, an animal, or even an inanimate object, is its essential quality which God has created and continues to sustain: thus, in this respect, God has predetermined all events. But every creature also possesses a will, which operates freely within the framework of its natural powers.

Like the Stoics, Pelagius preached the highest moral standards, and in doing so he encouraged radical social reform also. He demanded that the wealthy should renounce their property, distributing it to the poor, keeping only enough back for the most basic needs. One of his close followers, another Briton, whose name remains unknown, wrote a tract which sent shock waves through the Roman establishment. In it he compared the rich man living in a mansion built out of white marble, to the poor in a hut of sticks and turfs. 'Did God will such inequality?' the writer asked. 'Does the poor man feel the sun less keenly than the rich? Should there be one law for the poor and another for the rich?' And he went on to castigate the rich for calling the poor 'a rabble' and 'miserable wretches', when it is the rich themselves who are truly wretched for disobeying God's commands. Pelagius also taught a strict sexual ethic in which celibacy is an ideal to which all should aspire. He did not condemn matrimony, but urged couples who no longer wanted more children to abstain from sexual relations in order to give themselves more wholly to God in prayer and acts of charity.

Pelagius believed that everyone was able to attain the perfection of Christ, and Pelagius's image of the perfect Christ-like person is similar to the Stoic man of wisdom. He should be indifferent to poverty and even humiliation, because his satisfaction arises from the inward knowledge that he is living in accordance with God's laws. He seeks to cause injury to no living creature, but to live in harmony with nature.

But if such an ideal had its origins in ancient Greek philosophy, it found its major Christian expression in the monastic movement. And as monasticism spread westward as far as Gaul and Britain in the fifth century, carried there by such men as John Cassian, so Pelagius's philosophy was readily adopted. Cassian called the commitment to the Christian life the 'step of faith', and this step depended entirely on the will of the individual, responding freely to the teachings of Christ. Like Pelagius, Cassian denied any notion of original sin, and instead emphasised that in every human heart there is the innate desire to obey the commandments of God; sin is the perversion of that desire for evil ends. It is thus a matter of personal choice as to whether we fulfil our natural potential for goodness, or whether we deny our own true nature. Such a robust belief in individual freedom seemed to Cassian the essential foundation of monastic life, for only if each monk was held responsible for his own actions, could the corporate discipline of the community be maintained.

47

Filling Empty Spaces

By the first decade of the fifth century Pelagius had gained a high reputation for the holiness of his personal life, and for the rigour of his teaching. And to most people his ideas seemed to pose no threat to the Christian faith, but seemed wholly in tune with the Scriptures. Yet many perceptive theologians recognised that Pelagius had brought to the surface an attitude to sin and salvation which, if followed to its logical conclusion, would strike at the heart of the Church's spiritual authority – and, as some saw it, at the authority of God himself.

Pelagius's chief opponent was Augustine, the most powerful theologian the Church had yet produced. The two men were approximately the same age, and they shared the same passionate desire for truth – combined with a furious intolerance of those who disagreed with their conception of truth. Augustine's mother Monica was a Christian, but in his early adult life Augustine was attracted to the Manichees, a flourishing sect which combined both pagan and Christian ideas. The Manichees taught a strict dualism, in which goodness and evil are independent powers engaged in constant battle. Augustine was obsessed with the problem of evil, especially sexual lust, and the Marichean image of the universe mirrored the war going on within him, between the desire for bodily pleasure and the call to the ascetic life of a monk. For nine years Augustine followed Manichean teaching, struggling to control his desires by the most harsh self-discipline. Frequently he lapsed, and through much of this period kept a mistress, but even when he succeeded in controlling himself, he found no peace. Eventually he rejected the Manichees and, to Monica's great joy, embraced Christianity.

During the next decade tracts poured from Augustine's pen denouncing the falsehood of the Manichees; and the Christian theology expressed in his works is remarkably close to that of Pelagius. In a book entitled *Against Fortunatus*

– Fortunatus being a Manichean leader in North Africa –
Augustine claimed 'there is no sin unless through one's own
will, and we do right things also by our will.' But gradually
his ideas swung back towards the Manichean philosophy,
although now the forces of good were firmly identified with
the Christian God. He no longer saw sin as the product of
human will, but as a power which enslaves the whole of
mankind. And it was only through divine grace, which the
individual can neither earn nor merit through his own efforts,
that a person could be saved.

The starting point of Augustine's theology of sin and salvation is Adam's first sin in the Garden of Eden. In Augustine's
eyes, Adam's sin was twofold: firstly pride, in wishing to be
independent from God's commands, and to decide for himself how to live; and secondly lust, which enslaved Adam at
the very moment when he thought he was gaining his freedom. Lust, which was originally the 'daughter of sin', now
became the 'mother of sin', causing Adam's corruption to be
passed from one generation to another through the sexual
act. Lust also spills over into every aspect of life, becoming
the 'selfish enjoyment of all material things, without reference to God'. Having inherited Adam's sin at birth, we are
incapable by our own will of resisting it. In the famous words
which Augustine quoted from an earlier writer, 'In Adam all
mankind sinned as a lump'.

It follows that God alone can redeem man, and that it
is entirely God's choice as to whether a particular person
is saved or damned. Athanasius had already developed the
idea that Christ's death was the debt of justice that mankind
had to pay to God for Adam's sin. In dying, Christ had
taken on himself the punishment that man deserved, and so
paved the way for God to redeem sinners. To this Augustine
added the novel idea that, from the total number of angels
in the heavenly city, a number had fallen away; and that, in
order to fill their places, God decided to save that number of
human beings. Thus, even before birth each person's destiny
had been planned by God, some to be saved by his grace and

taken up to the heavenly city to fill empty spaces, and the rest to be cast away. To those who objected to the injustice of condemning people before birth, Augustine replied that eternal damnation was what everybody deserved – and it is only through God's mercy that any are saved.

Despite the personal respect in which Pelagius was held, his ideas began to meet opposition among other clergy and theologians within Rome. They objected that if individuals could achieve perfection by their own efforts, not only was there no place for divine grace, but the sacraments of the Church were unnecessary too. Thus, it was argued, Pelagius's teaching would empty the churches. But the dispute was only brought to a head after the fall of Rome in 410, when Pelagius fled with thousands of others to North Africa. It was there that he encountered Augustine, now Bishop of Hippo, on the African coast. The two men probably met soon after Pelagius's arrival, for Augustine wrote warmly about Pelagius's sanctity. But, as Augustine became familiar with the teaching of Pelagius and his followers, he was aghast, for it contradicted all that he himself had come to believe. Unlike Rome, where Pelagius had enjoyed widespread support, North Africa was alien ground, and in 416 Augustine convened a Council of African bishops which condemned Pelagius for heresy.

There followed two years of confusion, during which the two camps tried to rally support in the wider Church. The African bishops wrote to Pope Innocent in Rome giving lengthy reasons for Pelagius's condemnation, and asking his approval. After six tense months Innocent replied, agreeing with only two of their points: that Pelagius's teaching was wrong to imply that petitionary prayer and infant baptism were unnecessary. To our knowledge Pelaguis had never spoken against infant baptism, although it is reasonable to suppose that in his view unbaptised infants would be saved, since they had been born in innocence rather than in sin. And, as for prayer, Pelagius had always given it a high place as the principal means by which grace enters our 'posse'.

None the less Innocent's letter was sufficient for Augustine to declare that 'The case is finished', and to hope that any lingering Pelagian tendencies would soon be swept away.

But Augustine was premature. Within a few weeks of writing his letter Innocent died, and his successor, Pope Zosimus, was an admirer of Pelagius. Moreover, one of Pelagius's closest followers travelled to Rome to reassure the new Pope that Pelagius's views were quite consistent with infant baptism, since baptism is a symbol of divine love rather than a means to salvation. Zosimus accepted this view as orthodox, and wrote to the Africans telling them that their condemnation of Pelaguis was based on a false representation of his teaching. Augustine was unimpressed, and promptly wrote to the eastern churches of Constantinople and Alexandria to ask for their support. Since they had long resented Rome's claims to be the centre of the universal Church, they gladly joined Augustine in the battle with the Pope. And in 418 a Council was held in Carthage, attended by over 200 bishops from throughout Christendom. Zosimus wilted under the pressure, and Pelagius's teaching was finally declared heretical. Pelagius himself died two years later, in lonely exile probably in some eastern desert.

In his greatest work, *The City of God*, written during the Pelagian controversy, Augustine portrayed the history of the universe as a battle between two invisible societies, of the elect and of the damned. The elect are filled with the love of God, which leads to a disregard of self, while the damned are motivated by the love of self, which leads to the disregard of God. Augustine was too subtle a thinker to indentify the society of the elect directly with the institutional Church; and he recognised that love of self is often vital for human society to function smoothly. But to many who read the book or heard its ideas at second hand, it was a clarion call for the Church to fight a tireless war against all who opposed her spiritual authority. And Augustine himself was convinced that even the slightest hint of individual freedom in spiritual matters threatened the very foundation of the Church. If Pelagius's view had prevailed, then the religious monopoly which the Church enjoyed for over 1,000 years would never have been sustained. But with Pelagius defeated, the medieval bishops could assert with confidence – as they did whenever their authority was called into question – that 'there is no salvation outside the Church'.

Model for Politics

Abelard's Logic

In a stable, unchanging society it is easy to assume that the traditional pattern of life reflects God's will, and that if people fulfil the duties and maintain the customs which society imposes, they are thereby obeying God. And in medieval Europe, despite numerous wars and occasional famines, no one doubted that the feudal system, with its strict hierarchy and complex web of mutual obligations, had been ordained by the Almighty. Equally the Church, with its own parallel hierarchy of Pope, bishops and priests, was regarded as God's creation, to uphold morality and dispense the sacraments. So, whenever people reflected upon divine salvation, it is small wonder that they readily accepted Augustine's view that just as the king could grant favours and the Pope could pronounce blessings, so in the final judgement God could freely choose whom to redeem and whom to damn. In the social, moral and spiritual realms alike, there was little scope for individual choice.

But the human spirit is never as quiescent as kings and bishops would like, and on the issue of salvation one rebellious soul, Peter Abelard, raised questions and offered answers that rocked the Church then – and has continued to shake the solid structure of orthodoxy ever since. Abelard was born in 1079, a generation later than Anselm, and was educated in Paris, where his fierce arguments with his teachers over abstruse points of philosophy marked him out as both a genius and a troublemaker. For a period he studied Anselm's philosophy at a theological school set up by Anselm's disciples, and was inspired by Anselm's intellectual courage in submitting every point of Christian doctrine to critical scrutiny. But clashes with his teachers forced him to leave and, returning to Paris, he became tutor to Heloise, the young daughter of a canon at Notre Dame called Fulbert. The passionate affair of the brilliant philosopher and his intelligent and devout pupil is the most famous love story of medieval Europe. A child was born, and Abelard and Heloise were secretly married, but Fulbert took his revenge by having Abelard emasculated. Heloise thereupon became a nun, eventually rising to be abbess of a convent.

Abelard too felt compelled to take monastic vows, joining the community at St Denis. But far from settling peacefully into the quiet routine, Abelard continued to stir up trouble. He made himself unpopular with his fellow monks by criticising the worldly comforts they enjoyed, and eventually was forced to leave. Worse still, the theological books he had been writing now attracted the fury of the Church authorities. He was deemed to be denying the doctrine of the Holy Trinity, and for the last twenty years of his life he faced frequent condemnation by bishops and abbots, with his books being collected and burnt in market squares throughout France. In 1141 he was branded a heretic by the Pope in Rome, and he died a year later.

The mainspring in Abelard's thought is his optimism about the power of human reason, both in understanding the natural order, and in penetrating the supernatural realm. Thus, he was convinced that pagan philosophers, such as Aristotle and Plato, had worked out in embryonic form many of the truths revealed later in Jesus Christ. Equally he believed that the Scriptures should be read with critical eyes, for, although inspired by God, they were composed by fallible authors, transmitted by fallible scribes, interpreted by fallible theologians – and, besides, language itself is always liable to be ambiguous. The most important of his own scriptural studies is his *Exposition of Romans*, which contains his famous arguments against the orthodox doctrine of redemption, and his own alternative theory.

Abelard begins by stating what he regards as orthodoxy: that through Adam's fall we are enslaved to the devil, and thus deserve punishment; and that by his death on the cross Christ suffered our punishment, and so allows God to save a certain portion of the human race. Abelard then peppers this doctrine with all manner of objections. Why should God have allowed the devil to enslave mankind? Why should the whole of mankind be threatened with punishment because of Adam's sin? How does Christ's death actually let us off that punishment? Is it not cruel and wicked that an innocent person should be crucified, to pay the price for another person's sin? And, last but not least, is it not monstrous that God should choose for salvation only a small minority of the human race, all equally sinful? None of these objections were new since Pelagius and his followers had raised similar issues hundreds of years earlier. But, while in Pelagius's time orthodoxy had not yet been clearly defined, Abelard was deliberately refuting the accepted teaching of the Church.

Abelard then offered his own solution. The obstacle to our redemption is neither the devil's dominion over us, nor God's need to inflict a punishment for Adam's sin; rather, it is that we ourselves are deficient in love. When Christ laid down his life, he demonstrated to us the fullness of love which we are all called to share; and, if we follow the example of his life and death, we too shall be 'bound to God in love'. Thus Christ's death on the cross 'wins for us the true liberty of the sons of God' by showing that we can 'do all things out of love, and not out of fear'.

It is small wonder that such a theory was regarded as dangerous and subversive. In Abelard's view bishops and priests could no longer sit comfortably in the belief that God had saved them. They, like everyone else, must strive to imitate the actions and attitudes of Christ. Worse still, by suggesting that anyone, even pagans, could be saved if they lived by the law of love, Abelard struck at the roots of the Church's spiritual monopoly. Not surprisingly, Abelard received scant support. Even the 'angelic doctor', Thomas Aquinas, who was as intelligent and penetrating as Abelard in his theology, re-stated the old orthodoxy on the question of redemption. His only criticism of Augustine's view was that the number of the elect is not determined by the vacancies left in heaven by the fallen angels, but is a matter of God's free choice.

It was, however, the Protestant Reformers, Luther and Calvin, who most vigorously refuted Abelard and championed Augustine. The spirit behind the Reformation was one of freedom. People wanted to shake lose the shackles of age-old customs and obligations, in order to create new economic and social systems. Also, they yearned to study the Scriptures for themselves and to enter a direct relationship with God, without the mediation of finely dressed priests and elaborate rituals. Yet when it came to redemption and salvation, the reformers insisted that Christianity retained its monopoly. Calvin, who was always crystal clear in his teaching, wrote that Christ died on the cross, not for all mankind, but only for the elect: hence, some are predestined for salvation, and some for eternal destruction. If anyone cavilled at God's apparent injustice, Calvin repeated Augustine's answer that everyone deserves to be punished for their sins. For those who had faith in Christ, Calvin's doctrine was most reassuring, particularly when he added that the Spirit 'reveals to our minds and confirms to our hearts' that we are saved. But for those with no knowledge of Christ, and for those filled with doubt, the fires of hell beckoned.

Both Calvin and Luther were aware that their teaching could undermine morality: that, since a person's outward behaviour could have no affect on the destiny of his soul, there was nothing to deter moral licence. Calvin's solution to this conundrum was that the man who was saved would automatically be upright and sober in his actions, and that immorality was a sure sign of damnation. Within the strict religious atmosphere of Calvin's holy city, Geneva, such a warning sufficed. But Calvin and Luther had unwittingly driven a thick wedge between Augustine's two cities. Membership of God's city was purely a matter of divine choice, and no effort to be loving towards one's neighbours could win a place; so the Church had no business in offering moral guidance to society as a whole. In the world of political and economic affairs, the devil's writ runs, and the saved and the damned alike must compete to survive. Thus, as Luther saw clearly, kings and princes cannot depend on moral laws to maintain order, but must rule by fear.

Pleasure and Love

There was now a moral vacuum in society. For a millenium, the Church had been the moral guardian of every aspect of social and political life, and even when its authority had been flouted by greedy kings and emperors, its right to give moral commands had never been doubted. Now, however, the Reformers had – without intending to do so – repudiated that right. At the same time the social order itself was undergoing a revolution. A new merchant class was rising throughout Europe, and old feudal obligations were being swept aside by the forces of capitalism; even the humblest peasant found himself growing crops and weaving cloth, not for his own needs, but to sell in the market. In the late middle ages, in the early stages of this revolution, the Church sought to guide the merchants, telling them how to set their prices and in what circumstances they could charge interest on loans. Calvin himself tried to stipulate an upper limit on the interest which the wealthy bankers of Geneva could demand. But the rest of his theology gave little authority to such pronouncements, and after his death the moral reins on capitalism were finally broken.

Into this vacuum came an entirely new approach to

morality. Throughout the medieval period the source of moral authority was God's law, as conveyed through Scripture and the Church; and the purpose of morality was to transform humanity into the image of Christ. In the seventeenth century a new breed of philosophers asserted that morality could only be derived from the nature of man himself, and that the purpose of every action should be to satisfy our innate wants and needs. Thus the focus of ethics shifted from theology to psychology. The more extreme proponents of this approach, such as Thomas Hobbes, argued that human wants are entirely selfish, each individual seeking only to maximise his own pleasure and minimise his pain. As Jeremy Bentham put it a century later, all notions of 'right' and 'wrong' can be reduced to a simple calculation of pleasure and pain: a man calls an action 'right' if it increases pleasure, and 'wrong' if it increases the pain. Others, especially those like Shaftesbury, who regarded themselves as Christian, asserted that amongst our desires is a natural 'benevolence' which causes us to sympathise with the pain and deprivation of others: thus, enlightened self-interest will lead human beings to act charitably.

A compromise between these two positions was proposed by the moralist and economist, Adam Smith, in the late eighteenth century, and his view is now the common moral attitude throughout the western world. He saw human life as divided into two spheres, the personal and the political. In personal relationships, such as within the family or amongst friends, we are naturally concerned with the needs of others, and our innate 'moral sense' will induce us to sacrifice our own wants to theirs. But in political and economic relationships, self-interest rules. When we go to the baker we do not expect charity, but exchange money for bread because both gain from the transaction. And when we invest our capital or seek employment, we look not how best to serve others, but how to maximise our income. Smith sought to demonstrate how, in matters of political economy, the free market, in which each person freely pursues his own interests, will lead to the greatest good for all, and he spoke of an 'Invisible Hand' by which the selfish actions of individuals become the means of increasing the whole nation's prosperity.

On the face of it, Smith's compromise left a place for Christianity, albeit rather restricted. Within the private sphere, the Church could present itself as the guardian of family life and the exponent of charitable activities. And in the nineteenth century, when Britain and other European nations set out to colonise the world, capitalism and Christianity were regarded as partners, the former to bring prosperity and political stability, the latter to instill morality and save souls. But, as the modern philosopher MacIntyre has observed, the entire approach of Smith, and even of Shaftesbury, undermined any kind of Christian morality. Christianity, in common with every religion, is concerned with moral and spiritual progress, from a state of sin or ignorance, towards greater goodness and enlightenment. Hence, if our innate wants and needs are regarded as the basis of morality, there is no place for religion.

Christianity, throughout the nineteenth and twentieth centuries, has thus found itself in a moral quandary. And amongst Christian moralists there have been two, diametrically opposed, responses. The first has been to build on Smith, or rather Shaftesbury, in taking human nature as the starting point, and to see if the seeds of Christian morality can be found within the human soul. In its boldest form it has led to the 'situation ethics' of the philosopher Fletcher. He asserts that love is a natural human attribute, which Christianity elevates to the status of a guiding principle for all human conduct. He sees no place for absolute moral laws, since no law can directly define the loving action in every circumstance. Instead, each situation must be assessed on its own merits, and the individuals involved should work out how love can be maximised. Love in this scheme is thus very similar to Shaftesbury's 'benevolence': it is our natural propensity to do good to others.

The Call to Heresy

The opposite response is to go back to Calvin and Luther, and to seek divine moral laws which are binding on Christians. Although the Reformers' scheme of salvation gave little incentive to moral action, they firmly believed that Christians should live by the highest moral standards as an outward sign of God's saving grace, and that these were to be found in the Bible. Today, following Calvin and Luther, many Christians thumb through their Bibles seeking precise moral guidance about every aspect of life. In some extreme groups this involves giving equal weight to every biblical commandment, from Christ's teaching about forgiveness to Paul's prohibition about women speaking in church. Other more moderate groups try to make a distinction between permanent laws, and those which applied only in the New Testament times: thus, typically, laws about dress are ignored, while sexual commands about fornication and homosexuality are regarded as binding. While in a wholly Christian society, such as Calvin's Geneva, a purely Biblical approach to mortality can command widespread assent, in modern western countries it inevitably creates a gulf between Christians and the rest; thus it prevents Christianity from giving any moral lead to society as a whole.

There is, however, an important variation in the biblical approach, which has its origins in the evangelicals of the eighteenth century. It is often forgotten today that John Wesley and his followers incurred the violent condemnation, not only of complacent bishops, but also of most orthodox Protestants. Wesley rejected the doctrine of Calvin and Luther that only a predestined elect should be saved, and preached that salvation was open to everyone. He criss-crossed the country, and toured the world, inviting humble peasants and richer landowners alike to accept God's loving grace into their hearts. An Anglican bishop might spit at his 'enthusiasm', but to the Puritans Wesley was a heretic. Wesley himself gave little attention to morality – although he himself was immensely generous to anyone in need – but it was not long before his followers realised that Wesley's teaching implied an entirely new attitude to social and political issues, as well as to moral questions. The salvation of a man's soul could not, they realised, be separated from the material conditions in which he lived: if a man dwelled in a degrading overcrowded slum, and worked in a vast impersonal factory, or, worse still, was unemployed with no hope of improving his lot, then he would be deaf to the gospel of love.

So through the nineteenth century, evangelical Christians campaigned for new laws, started national charities, ran schools and hospitals, and even built new towns, to raise the living standards of the working-classes. Perhaps the most famous of these philanthropists was General Booth, founder of the Salvation Army. He spent his early years, like Wesley, preaching the Gospel, and trying to win souls for Christ. But gradually he realised that the industrial cities of the western world were teeming with millions of people for whom the daily struggle for survival was destroying their souls as well as their bodies. Thus, he concluded that the mission of Christianity is to bring both 'heavenly hope and earthly blessings to the hearts of the multitudes.' And, in such a conviction, the Salvation Army has for a century worked to improve the lot of the poorest of the poor.

Booth's vision was remarkably similar to that of the Christian Socialist leader, F. D. Maurice. He believed that industrial capitalism was alienating people from one another, and hence closing their hearts to the law of love: 'The doctrine of competition makes it impossible for the employer to look upon his worker except as one who is wanting wages he is not disposed to give; or the worker to look upon his employer except as one who is offering wages upon which he cannot exist.' He proclaimed that 'God's voice has gone forth clearly bidding us to come forward to fight against the present state of things,' calling us to recognise our 'common creation, common redemption and common humanity . . . which are the primary eternal bonds upon which all others depend.' Thus, for Booth and Maurice alike, the Church's mission is twofold: it is evangelistic, urging individuals to repent of their sins, and follow Christ; and it is prophetic, calling on society to transform its morality and its social system, so that all can share in the blessings of God.

Thy Kingdom Come

Christian morality, and, less obviously, the Christian doctrine of salvation, are in a muddle, Few now believe in Augustine's doctrine of predestination, although it remains firmly rooted in most catechisms; and most would go some, if not all, the way into Pelagius's camp. But our ideas about morality and salvation have been influenced so deeply by Augustine, over so many centuries, that we cannot escape the effects of his teaching. The Protestant Reformers, in adopting almost wholesale Augustine's scheme, created an unbridgeable gulf between Christian and secular morality. Thus Christians have to choose on which side of the gulf to stand. Some, like the exponents of situation ethics, have placed themselves firmly on the secular side, seeking to give a Christian gloss to prevailing moral attitudes. Others walk proudly on the Christian bank, distilling from Scripture divine laws by which to lead their lives. Most, however, adopt the moral schizophrenia of Adam Smith: on private matters, such as sexuality, they follow the biblical laws, but on social and political issues their outlook is secular.

But Augustine has never held the entire field. Pelagius himself may have been condemned, but, in a very different theological arena, his ideas found expression in Abelard. And, in recent centuries, both the Evangelical Revival and the Christian Socialist movement have, in their various ways, been a Pelagian rebellion against Augustinian orthodoxy. Pelagius and Abelard taught that salvation ultimately depends on individual choice: Jesus Christ demonstrated for us the way of salvation, and it is for each individual to decide whether to follow him. And this is not only a spiritual, but also a moral choice: the person who wants to be saved must change every aspect of his life, from how he conducts his personal relationships to how he spends his money. The Evangelicals and the Christian Socialists took this one stage further into the field of politics: Christian conversion demands not only a high standard of personal morality, but also a change in political and social institutions, to enable people to grow in love.

The implications for the Church of adopting a Pelagian theology are enormous. At the level of faith it encourages, even demands, an Arian view of Christ which stresses his humanity. The fundamental reason for the condemnation of Arius was that if God's punishment for the sin of Adam was to be born by a single individual, only a divine person was sufficient. But if this view of redemption is rejected, then the contorted Chalcedonian formula about the two natures of Christ can be cast aside as well. Abelard's theory of redemption, by contrast, requires that Christ shared all our temptations and knew our weaknesses: only a person who was fully human could truly be an example for us to follow. This doctrine does not deny that Christ was in some way divine, but rather it leaves his divinity as a mystery beyond our grasp: what matters is that he was human, like us.

At the level of morality, Pelagius cuts through the muddle and sets us on a firm, clear course. Christianity has no place for secular morality based solely on human wants and needs, even if Shaftesbury's 'benevolence' is counted amongst those wants. Equally, man should not be turned into an unthinking slave to divine laws, since God does not want slaves, but free beings to give their consent to him in love. Rather, the purpose of morality is to unite the material and spiritual sides of our nature, satisfying our material needs, and enabling us to fulfil our spiritual potential. The teachings and example of Christ show us the spiritual stature which each of us is called to attain, and God is offering us the grace to grow in Christ's image. This potential is inherent in the nature of man, and only by fulfilling it we can achieve true joy and peace; so, to this extent, Christianity accords with Shaftesbury and others, who want to make human nature the foundation of morality. But, on the other hand, in fulfilling his potential, man transcends his own nature, his ordinary wants and needs being transformed by the power of divine love.

Most important of all, a Pelagian theology overturns our conventional approach to Christian mission. A pure Augustinian view leaves little place for mission, since the number of elect is already ordained. Pelagius, however, puts mission at the very heart of the Christian faith. The disciple of Christ is eager to share his joy with others, knowing that anyone who wishes to follow Christ can be saved; and the Church as a whole will want to change society, to give everyone the opportunity to grow in love. Thus evangelism and prophecy go hand in hand: the Church invites as many people as possible to come and join her ranks, and through their way of life and their preaching they become witnesses to God's kingdom on earth.

Pelagius was a fiery critic of the injustice and the oppression of the Roman Empire; and his later followers set up monasteries as living testimonies of how society should be ordered. Thus, in their time, the Pelagian monks were true prophets. A millennium and a half later, the Evangelicals and the Christian Socialists were fired by the same prophetic vision. The Christian Socialists created communities, not of monks, but of workers: in the slums of London they set up co-operatives in which men could work together in close fellowship, and share their common profits. Evangelicals also set up communities in the form of schools, hospitals and orphanages, and they were unashamedly political, fighting to make the Christian voice heard at every level of government.

How can we be prophets today? How can we think Christ's thoughts, proclaim his prophetic message, and live his prophetic life in the late twentieth century? We must begin, as Pelagius did, by being blunt and honest about our own sinfulness, and create for ourselves a pattern of life which is righteous – which enables us to grow in Christ's love. And this, as Pelagius and his followers saw clearly, means being part of a vibrant Christian community, in which the Gospel is put in a daily practice. Then, like Pelagius, and like the Evangelicals and Christian Socialists, we will have the authority to speak from our own experience about how society itself can be transformed. Inevitably, we shall find ourselves talking about political and economic issues, because God's kingdom on earth must embrace everything which affects people's attitudes and actions; and, inevitably, some will regard us as subverting the social order because, like all prophetic movements, our pattern of life will be revolutionary in its implications.

Our mission will thus unite Augustine's two cities. For him the city of God, and the city of man's secular activities, were entirely separate, each with its own values. Our task is to push back the frontiers of God's city until it embraces the whole secular world. F. D. Maurice wrote that 'Christ came to establish a kingdom, in which God will reign over the body politic, the laws that governments enact, the work that people do, every relationship which they enter'. Maurice saw the task of theology and of mission as 'digging for God's kingdom' to reveal that 'economy and politics have firm divine ground beneath themselves'. The economic, political and social insights which Christians can offer the world will vary from century to century, even from year to year, as society evolves and circumstances change. Thus, as Maurice saw clearly, there is not a 'single political system' which Christianity must espouse. But the values, proclaimed in Christ's teachings and embodied in his life, are eternal, and the Church is called to embody these values in its own corporate life, and thence proclaim them to the world.

The Christian community – the Church – is thus called

to be the city of God on earth; and its way of worship and its style of ministry must directly reflect the message which it seeks to proclaim. This was the passionate concern of an older contemporary of Pelagius, called Donatus, who also incurred Augustine's wrath – and who is the heretical hero of our next chapter.

Part 3
Donatus

Jesus the Charismatic

The First Charismatic

Throughout the history of the Church, Christians have argued about how they should organise themselves. Whilst most people soon get lost in the complex maze of Christian doctrine, everyone can distinguish one form of organisation from another – and hence have strong views as to which is best. As a consequence, Christians have often split apart on this question, naming their denomination according to its structure of leadership: Presbyterian churches are those run by local presbyters, Congregational churches are democratic with the whole membership taking decisions, Episcopal churches are centralised with bishops in charge, and, of course, the Roman Catholic Church is so named because the Pope in Rome is its leader.

Within two or three decades of Christ's death, the organisation and leadership of the Church was emerging as a major bone of contention, and the pages of the New Testament show that issues that still divide us today were hotly debated by the first Christians. Paul encouraged a charismatic pattern of leadership in his churches, in which every member exercised a ministry according to his gifts. His list of ministries include apostles and prophets, teachers and evangelists, administrators and healers; and he believed that the Spirit would provide whatever gifts the Church needed. The church which most successfully embodied Paul's vision was that in Corinth, but it was here too that Paul became most acutely aware of the problems. Charismatic churches, then as now, are notoriously prone to division, with different groups claiming

69

the direct guidance of the Spirit; thus the Corinthians split into at least three sects, each with its own leader. Paul pleaded for unity, and urged that every ministry should be tested to see whether it affirmed the lordship of Christ; but since his own authority as an apostle was itself under question, his words fell largely on deaf ears.

The church in Jerusalem, by contrast, was more hierarchical. From the outset it was led by the apostles who had been picked by Jesus himself; and the vacancy caused by Judas's desertion was filled by drawing lots. When the church became too large for the apostles to manage, and squabbles broke out over the distribution of funds, they appointed seven helpers to supervise the material aspects of its life. At this early stage there was considerable freedom, with the individuals who had received the Holy Spirit being encouraged to testify to others; and it was the whole congregation that chose the seven helpers, whom the apostles then ordained. It is not until the later pastoral epistles, addressed to Timothy and Titus, that something approaching an episcopal form of organisation emerges. Timothy seems to have been ordained to serve as leader of a number of churches; and his task was to teach the sound doctrine which had been passed to him, and maintain strict control over the moral and spiritual life of the congregations. If the Corinthian church seems somewhat wild and chaotic, Timothy's churches appear dull and stultifying by comparison.

By the second century, as Christianity spread throughout the Roman Empire, the great majority of churches were ruled by bishops, who exercised power over both spiritual and temporal affairs. In a letter of St Ignatius of Antioch written in the first decade of the century, we hear of three orders of ministry, with bishops at the top in charge of a group of churches, and local presbyters and deacons beneath them. He urged Christians to 'obey your bishop as if he were Jesus Christ', and pronounced that 'nobody should do anything with regard to the church without the bishop's approval.' Other writers, such as the compiler of the Didache, stressed that bishops should be chosen for their moral and spiritual qualities – they should be 'meek and not lovers of money, true and reliable' – but made clear that all the various ministries described by Paul were now exercised solely by the local bishop, and those serving under him. For some decades the actual choice of bishops remained in the hands of the people, but as bishops themselves became organised into a hierarchy, with one diocese taking precedence over another, the patriarchs of the major cities appointed men to dioceses within their province.

But as the Church grew more rigid and authoritarian, so there was an inevitable reaction, with people yearning for the charismatic freedom of Paul's congregations. In the latter half of the second century, a Christian convert in Asia Minor, called Montanus, declared himself to be a prophet, directly guided by the Holy Spirit. He taught that every Christian could receive divine inspiration, so that the whole Church would become 'like a lyre, with the Spirit playing upon her like a plectrum'. Montanus gained a large following, especially in the rural areas of Asia Minor, and entire villages and towns adopted 'the new prophecy', as it became known. In addition to believing in direct inspiration, the Montanists insisted on the most rigorous moral standards, with lengthy fasts being required as penance for even the smallest lapse. Montanus' worship was marked by ecstatic singing and even dancing, with every member being free to preach and prophesy as they felt moved. One might have expected the bishops to have stamped out the movement; but many bishops admired its spiritual zeal, and for two decades it spread unchecked.

By about 180, Montanus groups were forming as far west as Gaul and Carthage; and it was in North Africa that the movement gained its most powerful advocate, Tertullian. Brought up by pagan parents, Tertullian studied law and philosophy, and his writings display an immense knowledge of classical literature. He had a fiery and passionate temperament, and was deeply impressed by the heroism of the Christians under persecution. In his late twenties he himself became a Christian, and thereafter was a scourge of both decadent pagan society and also the moral laxity or many Christians. His numerous tracts bristle with righteous anger. He regarded the Roman Empire as the work of the devil, and saw the Church as the embryo of the new social order which God was creating. Thus there was no room for compromise with the world: Christians must be pure, 'with neither a spot nor wrinkle', foregoing all material luxuries such as fine food and clothes, and refusing military service. And all who lapse must ruthlessly be cast out. Amongst his circle were Perpetua, a young married woman, and her slave Felicitas who, in 203, were arrested for their faith; their courageous joy as they were thrown to the lions in the Carthage amphitheatre has since been depicted in countless paintings.

Tertullian himself escaped arrest and lived to old age, but in his last twenty years his main battle was not with the pagan authorities, but with the church in Rome. Tertullian had two major quarrels. Firstly he loathed the tendency in Rome, and elsewhere, to emphasise the divinity of Christ at the expense of his humanity. This was not merely a theological question, but it affected the entire practice of Christian faith. The birth of Jesus in a draughty stable, his work as a humble carpenter, his ministry amongst the sick and vulnerable, and his death as a criminal, expressed for Tertullian the suffering and humility that all Christians are called to share. So when comfortable clergy in Rome – as Tertullian saw it – turned Christianity into a set of elaborate rituals, and Christ into a remote divine figure, Tertullian saw the foundations being knocked from beneath the faith.

It was his second quarrel, however, which finally allied him with Montanism. Rome's moral discipline, Tertullian asserted, was weak and cowardly, allowing all sorts of moral diseases to infect 'the bride of Christ'; and this weakness arose from a denial of the Holy Spirit as the direct source of guidance and courage for all Christians. For most of his life, Tertullian sought to remain in communion with Rome; but finally his patience was exhausted, and he joined the New Prophecy.

Montanism in Asia Minor, having flourished without hindrance for twenty years, was finally declared heretical in 177, at roughly the time it was spreading to the west. Tertullian, in joining the sect, was thus breaking from orthodoxy. But the ideals which inspired Montanism and Tertullian were not quashed, and have continued to bubble up in the Church throughout the centuries. The next, and perhaps greatest, eruption of charismatic Christianity was also in North Africa, a century later, under the venerable bishop Donatus.

The First Revival

In Tertullian's time, the church in Carthage was still quite small, and he could plausibly regard it as a school, composed of convinced and dedicated individuals who were guiding one another in the way of Christ. But in the first half of the third century, the North African church expanded rapidly, and by the time the wealthy Cyprian became bishop in 248, the evangelical fire of earlier times had cooled into cautious pragmatism. Cyprian believed strongly in the authority of bishops, and was suspicious of any claims to direct inspiration. He was willing to welcome back into the church moral backsliders if they underwent some form of penance. Thus the church of Carthage was now little different from its sister church in Rome, which Tertullian had so despised.

Yet the rigour of Tertullian had not been wholly forgotten, and, to his dismay, Cyprian soon found himself drifting into conflict with Rome on the very issue which had forced Tertullian to break ranks. Even if Cyprian was willing to have backsliders as lay people in the church, he believed that the priests should be pure and blameless; and that not only were the sacraments administrated by a sinful priest invalid, but, worse still, they infected with sin those who received them. Rome, in the person of its bishop Stephen, taught that the efficacy of the sacraments depended entirely on the spiritual state of the recipients, so the morality of the priest was irrelevant. There was, in addition, a fresh dispute concerning church order. Both Cyprian and Stephen believed that the Holy Spirit guided the Church through her bishops; but while Cyprian thought the Spirit worked through the bishops meeting in council, Stephen asserted that the Bishop of Rome, as successor to Peter, had unique authority to settle doctrinal disputes. The issue has, of course, exploded intermittently down the centuries: and it was about to cause Cyprian and the church of Carthage to break with Rome, with Cyprian declaring Stephen a 'tyrannical heretic', and Stephen denouncing Cyprian as a 'false Christ', when, in 257, Stephen died. A year later, during renewed persecution, Cyprian was arrested and executed as 'ringleader of an unlawful association'.

The next half century saw relative calm between Rome and North Africa, but the conflict erupted again in the aftermath of the final persecution of the Emperor Diocletian. In 311 an ambitious archdeacon called Caecilian, by a wily manoeuvre, managed to install himself as bishop of Carthage. There was an immediate popular outcry against him as he was believed to have betrayed the faith to escape execution. The opposition was led by Donatus, a man who combined the skill of a politician with the sanctity of a hermit. He insisted that lapsed clergy, including Caecilian, should be deprived of their orders, and only re-admitted into the church as laymen if they were baptised afresh by a 'pure' priest. When, a year later, Constantine became Emperor, Caecilian supporters sought his backing; and,

Constantine, basing himself on reports which exaggerated the popularity of Caecilian, came down in his favour. To Constantine's horror, riots broke out in the streets of Carthage against his judgement. There followed a series of commissions, led by the bishops from other provinces, to try to settle the dispute, culminating in the Council of Arles in 314 (the first Church gathering, incidentally, at which the presence of British bishops is reported). Shocked by the fanaticism of Donatus's followers, the Council found in favour of Caecilian.

Yet, far from putting out the fire, this merely fanned the flames, with the majority of churches in Africa taking Donatus's side. Finally, in 317, Constantine felt compelled to use force, thus betraying his own edict made in Milan four years earlier promising religious freedom. Far from catching the Donatists by surprise, this was what they had expected. The had always regarded Constantine's support of Christianity as a political ploy to win approval in Rome; and since most North Africans regarded the Roman church as guided by Satan, Constantine was tarred with the same brush. Thus Constantine, the first Christian ruler, set an example which numerous Christian kings and emperors have followed since, of persecuting their unorthodox subjects.

From now onwards there were two separate churches in Africa, each with their own bishops and clergy: a small Catholic church in communion with Rome, confined mainly to the cities; and a much larger church, with Donatus as senior bishop, enjoying mass support in both the towns and the remote rural areas. Most Donatists believed that true Christianity was only to be found in Africa, the rest of the church having fallen away from the pure faith, and that their mission was to reconvert the world. Also, among many of the poorer peasants, Donatism expressed their hatred both of the imperial government, which extracted heavy taxes, and of the rich landlords who oppressed them. Thus the movement, like so many Christian movements since that time, combined social protest with spiritual zeal.

The theology of Donatus and his followers was attractively simple. While Rome and the Emperor sought the unity of the Church, at almost any spiritual price, the Donatists stressed its integrity. The true church, according to Donatus, is to be wholly committed to the teachings of Christ, even if this means casting out many who call themselves Christians. They believed that in baptism the convert is truly cleansed from sin, and thereafter has the grace to live a life of moral perfection; so when the convert emerges from the baptismal font, he is at that moment a new creation in Christ. Like the Montanists a century and a half earlier, the Donatists placed great emphasis on the guidance of the Holy Spirit, but while Montanus believed that the Spirit speaks only though individuals with the gift of prophecy, Donatus stressed that it is through groups of Christians seeking a common mind that the Spirit's voice is to be heard. Thus regular councils of clergy and bishops, discussing the issues of the day, were regarded as the essential tool of Church government.

The habit of defiance against the state authorities was so firmly rooted in African Christianity that Constantine's appeals for 'brotherly love' between Catholic and Donatist were bound to fall on deaf ears. But it was not violent confrontation which the Donatists sought; on the contrary, they were pacifists, believing that Christians should never take up arms. Their revolution was moral and spiritual, unmasking the false values of a militaristic government by joyfully accepting martyrdom at its hands. It was this, above all, that infuriated both Constantine and the Catholic bishops. At the Council of Arles, the bishops had rescinded the prohibition of Christians becoming soldiers, since the state itself now purported to be Christian; thus the Donatists' refusal to join the imperial army was an affront to the Emperor himself. But to the Donatists the very notion of a Christian state was a contradiction: until God himself reigns on earth, politics will always fall short of the divine ideal; and so the Church must always stand apart from the state, speaking out against its injustices.

The Donatists built churches even in the remotest villages on the edge of the Sahara, as well as in the towns. The churches were usually bare and simple, with a huge font in which converts were totally immersed at baptism. Under the altar there was a stone trough in which were placed cooking pots containing relics of a martyr. Unlike the formal and sober worship of the Catholic churches, the Donatist congregations loved loud hymns which were sung in a full-throated roar. And at the heart of every service was a reading from the Bible, followed by an exposition of its meaning: in common with every reform movement since that time, the Donatists saw themselves as returning to the primitive roots of Christianity, as revealed in Scripture. After the Eucharist the Donatists typically enjoyed a meal together – an 'agape' – like the first Christians in Jerusalem.

Catholic Triumph

The dispute between Catholic and Donatist rumbled on throughout the fourth century, a constant irritant to the imperial government. Donatus himself made a fatal mistake in 346 when he travelled to Rome, believing that the Emperor would be sympathetic to his case. He asked if the Catholic bishops could be deposed, and he himself declared sole bishop of Carthage; the Emperor refused, and had Donatus arrested and exiled to Gaul, where he died in 355. The Donatists, however, survived this crisis, as well as a nasty scandal in which one of their bishops was unmasked as an adulterer and a cheat.

But in the dying years of the Roman Empire two factors combined to undermine the Donatists' power. The first was a rebellion in 397 led by an African feudal lord called

Gildo. He sought to exploit the weakness of the imperial
government, which was fighting invaders on all sides of its
great empire; and his ambition was to create an independent African state under his rule. A number of Donatist
leaders supported Gildo, aided by bands of peasants who
hoped that under Gildo their taxes would be reduced.
But Gildo's own brother Mascezel turned against him,
denouncing him as a profiteering tyrant, and other Donatist
leaders and peasants rallied to Mascezel's side. Mascezel,
with imperial help, easily defeated Gildo, and the rebellion
was quashed. In the process, however, the Donatist church
became divided, and, worse still, it had forfeited its claims
to moral superiority by becoming involved in military and
political affairs. Thus it was manifestly as blemished as the
Catholics by worldly sin.

The second, and ultimately decisive, blow to the
Donatists was the appearance of Augustine on the African
scene. Though African by birth, Augustine had spent most
of his early adult life in Rome and Milan; but in 393
the Catholic bishop of Carthage invited Augustine back
to Africa, and three years later consecrated him as bishop
of Hippo. Augustine's years in Italy had made him a loyal
Catholic; and, although in other circumstances he would
have been sympathetic with many of Donatus's ideas, he
now sought to destroy them with all the intellectual and
political skill he could command. In 397 he fired his first
salvo, a tract boldly entitled *Against the Heretic Donatus* and
in the wake of Gildo's abortive revolt, Augustine tirelessly
travelled round Donatus's churches trying to convince the
laity of their error. He also challenged Donatus's bishops
to open debate with him, to determine which was the true
Christian church in Africa; frightened of his rhetorical
skills, the Donatists refused, and lost the respect of many
educated Christians in the cities.

Augustine had three main arguments against the
Donatists. Firstly the unity – and the universality –
of the Church was more important than its spiritual

and moral integrity. Jesus Christ, Augustine asserted, had founded a worldwide Church, and, since the Roman Empire comprised almost all the known world, Augustine could argue that Christ's intention was now fulfilled. Hence the Donatists' claim that they alone were the true followers of Christ was patently absurd, since it implied that Christ's mission had been confined to Africa. Furthermore, Augustine said, the Donatists' position in effect excommunicated not only the church in Rome, but also the churches in such places as Ephesus and Antioch, founded by the apostles; and since the Donatists had no direct knowledge of these churches, they had no right to sever them from Christ's body.

Augustine's second argument followed from the first. The Christian mission was like a net cast into the sea bringing up every kind of fish, both good and bad, and it was for God alone on the Day of Judgement to divide one from the other. The Donatists, therefore, in trying to purify the church by casting out sinners, were thus arrogating to themselves God's authority – and hence were guilty of pride against God, which is the root of all human sin. Augustine believed that the 'City of God' was present on earth, made up of all those whom God had decided to save but this City was invisible, and should not be confused with the visible, institutional Church, which is only a distorted reflection of it.

The third argument concerned the thorny question of the sacraments. Donatus placed even greater importance on sacramental worship than did the Catholics; in particular, for the Donatists, baptism literally cleansed people from sin, whereas the more pragmatic Catholics saw it only as a symbol of purity. Yet it was not so much the meaning of the sacraments, but their administration, which divided the two sides. The Donatists stuck rigidly to their belief, inherited from Cyprian, that the sacraments were only valid and efficacious if administered by a priest who was spiritually pure; hence the priesthood must be constantly purged of sinners. To Augustine this constituted a double error. The priesthood, like the Church as a whole, will always consist of good and bad fish, and only God can distinguish with certainty between one and the other. More importantly, however, the validity of the sacraments depended not on the individual ministers, but on Christ himself, and the degree to which they are efficacious depends on the intentions of those receiving them. Thus a sinful priest cannot in any way compromise the sacraments.

These were all powerful arguments, and it is small wonder that the Donatists were reluctant to plead their case in public debate against such a weighty opponent. But soon Augustine was adding a fourth argument to the conflict, which was to have an incalculable effect on Christian attitudes in the succeeding centuries. Since the state authorities were Christian, Augustine asserted that the state should use its power to uphold orthodoxy and to punish heresy. Constantine, almost a century earlier, had set the example in his attempt to support Caecilian against Donatus; and now, Augustine believed, the state should act against Donatus's successors. Augustine acknowledged that he had come reluctantly to this view. As he wrote to a Donatist bishop, 'Originally my opinion was that no one could be coerced into the unity of Christ, that we must fight only by words . . . but I was convinced by the evidence within my own diocese, when people once on the side of Donatus were bought over to Catholic unity by the fear of imperial edicts.' He went on to use Christ's parable of the great banquet, where the master orders his servant 'to compel people to come in', to justify the use of force.

In 405, Donatism was officially outlawed, and persecution began. At first, while some of the wealthier Donatists in the cities came over to Catholicism, in the countryside people remained loyal to the Donatist priests. But six years later the Donatists, under threat of more severe measures, felt compelled to attend a grand conference of all the African bishops from both sides, to argue their respective cases before the Emperor's representative. The outcome was inevitable, as the Donatists were regarded by the imperial authorities as dangerous subversives. Thus on 30th January, an imperial edict was issued, banning the Donatist church, confiscating its property, and imposing heavy fines on those who refused to join the Catholic church. There was, however, to be no death sentence imposed on obstinate Donatists, since bitter experience had taught the authorities that creating martyrs only stiffened resistance.

At the heart of Augustine's faith, however, there was a paradox of which he himself was aware. Augustine by his own admission had been profoundly influenced by the Donatist theologian, Tyconius, who saw society divided into two conflicting cities, one owing allegiance to God and the other following Satan. The Donatists to a man saw themselves as belonging to God's city, and they identified the secular world of politics as Satan's city. Augustine adopted this Donatist image as the central theme of his greatest book, the *City of God*, and like the Donatists saw the Church's mission as a tireless struggle against the greed and corruption of the world. The difference lay in the social and political implications of that image. The Donatists believed that a pure church, true to its Christian mission, would always be an affront to the political order, and they accepted persecution as their inevitable lot. Augustine, however, recognised that in the world, law and order must be enforced to prevent human sin from reducing society to violent chaos. And if one section of the Church itself is a cause of disorder – as Augustine believed Donatists to be – then they must be quashed. A thousand years later this paradox was to haunt the Protestant reformers, who wanted to purify the Church by allowing the Holy Spirit to renew her worship and ministry, and yet at the same time supported the authority of governments to put down rebellion – even rebellion inspired by Christian principles.

81

Model for Ministry

Fox's Light

The outlawing of Donatus and his followers did not finally quell the charismatic spirit. As the Donatists found themselves banished to remote desert villages, so in another distant corner of the globe a new church was springing up, which was to be a thorn in the papal side for a further two centuries. In about 430 the Pope sent Palladius to Ireland to bring the tiny church there under his rule. Palladius loathed its cold, damp climate, and the Irish hated his haughty, condescending manner, and so a year later he returned to the comforts of Rome. He was replaced by Patrick, a British Christian who shared the same Celtic blood as the Irish, but who had been trained in Gaul. Patrick was enormously successful in making converts for Christ, but was himself converted to a style of Christianity quite alien to that of Rome. Its focus was monastism, and by the time of Patrick's death there was a network of monasteries and convents throughout Ireland. And in the following century, monks and nuns from these communities carried the Gospel and their way of life to Scotland, northern England, Wales, and thence even to Brittany.

The rugged Celtic Christians had no place for bishops living in grand palaces, or priests wielding power over their lives; and they had no towns in which to build grand churches or cathedrals. Nor did they have the patience or sophistication to debate the finer points of theology. The common people lived in scattered farmsteads, and were ruled by tribal chiefs who rode out from their hill-top fortresses. Chiefs and people alike wanted a simple and practical church that cared for people when they were sick and offered food and shelter to travellers, gave clear moral guidance and advice, and which, above all, enabled everyone to hear the words of Jesus for themselves, and so communicate directly with God. The monks and nuns, cloistered together in their beehive huts, could provide all this. Briget, Patrick's younger contemporary, was famed for walking each night along the highways near her convent to offer hospitality to wayfarers, and her infirmary was always filled with the old and sick from miles around. The monks, who went out to the farmsteads, taught the sayings and parables of Jesus without embellishment, encouraging people to follow the way of Christ without compromise. And the 'pilgrims' – the wandering monks – composed ballads which related the stories of the Bible in words that everyone could understand. There was no hierarchy, and every individual was regarded as responsible before God for his own salvation.

Pope after pope despaired of bringing these stubborn, uncivilised people under episcopal rule, condemning them as 'incurably Pelagian' – as indeed they were. Finally, in the seventh century at the Synod of Whitby, under great political pressure, the Celts of northern England submitted to Rome; and gradually, during the following 200 years, the rest of the British Isles followed. Yet even if the outward forms of the Celtic church disappeared, the inward spirit could not easily be quashed, and British Christianity continued to nuture strong-willed independent souls, such as Wulfstan who taught Canute the art of Christian kingship, and the gentle, but defiant, mystic Mother Julian. But it was in the wake of the Reformation that a wandering teacher emerged whose vision and way of life would have fitted perfectly amongst the Celtic saints. His name was George Fox, and by the time of his death one-in-a-hundred people in Britain followed his Celtic brand of religion – and he even had admirers amongst the Red Indian tribes in America.

He was born in 1624, the son of a weaver in a remote

Leicestershire village. His parents were Puritans, and he inherited their religious zeal. But by the age of nineteen he had concluded that all formal religion, Anglican and Puritan alike, was mere empty ritual, and he decided to 'walk solitary abroad' in search of the truth. For four years he visited priests and ministers, questioning them on their beliefs, but none gave answers that satisfied his soul. Then, one day in 1647, when he was on the brink of despair, he heard an inner voice say: 'There is One, even Christ Jesus, that can speak to thy condition.' These simple words had the force of divine revelation to him. They meant that he could converse directly with Christ, without need of religious teachers and books of theology. He described the voice of Christ speaking within the soul as 'the inner light', and was convinced that every person alive possessed this light, and all would see it if only they looked within their souls.

Thus the mission that occupied the rest of his life began: to urge people to seek the inner light, and to live by it. He started in north-western England, where the Anglican church was comparatively weak, and nonconformist groups of all kinds were flourishing. And soon his solitary mission was turning into a mass movement, with members from every class of society. He encouraged everyone – men and women, rich and poor, literate and ignorant – to preach and teach in the villages as they felt called. And when they met together for worship, he urged them to do the same, teaching one another as the inner light directed, and if no one was moved to speak, then they should sit in silence waiting on God. When in 1654, Fox decided to travel southwards to take his message into the heart of Anglican England, he was able to send groups of his followers ahead of him to distribute leaflets and convene meetings.

It was inevitable that his teaching should bring him into conflict with the Anglican church. He openly condemned the normal church service as 'meaningless babble', and he urged people to stay away from the 'steeple houses'. Worse still, he claimed that the bishops and ministers preached the

Gospel under false pretences. Their authority derived from the training they had received at university, where they had learned the minutiae of Christian doctrine. But to Fox no amount of intellectual study could add one jot to a person's Christian understanding; only direct spiritual experience could give a person the right to preach. On this Fox was at odds not only with the Church of England, but also with the ministers of the Puritan groups, who followed the teachings of the Swiss reformer Calvin. Calvin, while denying the authority of the Pope, had elevated the ordained ministry to a position of great power, enjoying the sole right to expound the truths of Christianity; and, to uphold this right, he had placed great emphasis on educating the ministers to the highest standard. In urging every true Christian to preach the Gospel, Fox was thus striking at the roots of the Protestant, Anglican and Catholic churches alike.

For a brief period under Cromwell, Fox was tolerated by the authorities. Cromwell needed the support of every dissenting religious group, and even at one point asked Fox to become a chaplain in his army. Fox refused, pronouncing that 'Christ's servants do not fight', since Christ has given us 'that life and power that takes away the occasion of all wars.' Rather than risk antagonising Fox's numerous followers, Cromwell ignored such defiance, and tried instead to undermine Fox by luring some of his closest companions into high political office. But this ploy also failed, and Cromwell was left lamenting that Fox and his followers could not be 'won by honours, high places and gifts as other people can.' Under Charles the Second, however, Fox soon became the target of vicious persecution. At first, in an effort to consolidate his power, King Charles tried to draw the dissenting religious groups back into the Church of England by offering doctrinal concessions. But, while many Puritans were ready to negotiate with the Anglican hierarchy, Fox would have none of it since his intention was to 'win people off from all the world's religions, which are vain, that they might know the true religion.'

During the following twenty years Fox suffered frequent spells in jail, and on occasions was tortured. This compelled him to set up a formal organisation to help his supporters to hold firm against attack. Some urged him to declare himself the national leader of a new religious society, but Fox bluntly rejected any such notion as this would have been a first step in creating the kind of hierarchy he despised. His concern was that his followers should remain free and equal, each enjoying the same status, and each able to minister to others as God directed. So he formed his followers into the Society of Friends, and in each locality set up a monthly meeting which all members were entitled to attend. Decisions were made by allowing everyone to speak as they felt moved, and thence seeking to form a consensus under the guidance of the Spirit. Votes were never taken, and resolutions only passed if they enjoyed unanimous support. Thus their meetings followed the pattern of their worship, with each member ministering to the whole.

Fox took his message abroad to Ireland, Holland and, most notably, to America where he won converts among both the Red Indians and the Colonists. But inevitably a religious group with so little formal leadership soon loses the coherence and efficiency of the more hierarchical churches. Within a generation or two of Fox's death the Quakers – as the society became popularly known – had become just another small sect, presenting little threat to the established church. Yet the challenge that his ideas represent to Christian life are embodied in almost every radical religious movement. A century after Fox, the Wesley brothers, though loyal Anglicans until their deaths, felt the same acute frustration with the self-satisfied hierarchy of the Church of England. The Methodist Society which they created – and which eventually split off to become a separate denomination – had a pattern of ministry which tried to incorporate a wide variety of different gifts. The minister, like Wesley himself, was a travelling evangelist, taking the Gospel to the ordinary people in factories and farms. The local groups had preachers, who expounded the Scriptures to those already converted. And in addition there were 'class leaders' who brought the members together in small groups in each other's homes, to share insights and to support one another in their various vocations. Thus, in its initial inception, Methodism was a more orderly version of Fox's Quakerism.

The fate of Methodism, to become in so many respects like the Anglican church from which it broke off, illustrates the perennial dilemma of Christian communities – how to sustain the charismatic style of ministry and worship, when the initial enthusiasm has worn off. The temptation is to regard charismatic communities as aberrations, which if necessary must be outlawed as heretical. Such was the fate of the Donatists, the Celts and the Quakers. But to do so is to fly in the face of the first apostles, whose communities in Jerusalem, Corinth, Rome and Ephesus were all charismatic in their ministry. And it is to condemn Christianity to a condition of dreary complacency.

The Search for Community

The great German sociologist, Max Weber, writing early in the twentieth century, described how religious institutions, when they are dying, erect giant bureaucracies. Each department of the bureaucracy will be concerned with some aspect of religion, such as mission, worship, social concern, morality and so on; and committees and conferences will compose reports and debate strategies on these issues. So all those involved will feel immensely busy, and imagine themselves to be most useful; but nothing will actually get done. Weber's theory was derived mainly from his observation of oriental religions, but it is depressingly close to what has occurred in the Christian churches in the West during the course of the twentieth century. Great ecclesiastical bureaucracies have come into being presided over by bishops whose way of life resembles that of a senior government official. A typical clergyman today may spend more of his time attending committees than visiting his flock, more hours filling in forms than composing sermons. Synods and councils debate resolutions and cast votes in pale imitation of a political parliament. And, as Weber predicted, all this has been accompanied by a steady drop in church attendance and Christian commitment.

Yet this is not the whole picture. As bureaucracies have grown and churches declined there have been three powerful movements within Christianity which are beginning to bear rich fruit. On the face of it these movements have quite different and, at times, divergent aims, and to the outside observer the picture may appear confused. The first is the ecumenical movement. Its founding father was the great Victorian theologian, F.D. Maurice, who in 1838 wrote a book entitled *The Kingdom of Christ*, in which he argued that all the various parties and sects in Christianity possess complementary gifts and ministries, and that if they joined together in a single institution, they would become a truly 'Catholic' church. He looked in depth at the denominations in England, discovering the particular insights and experiences which each could offer. And he urged them to form a united Church of England, which would itself be part of the worldwide Catholic Church. It was an inspiring and a noble vision, and ten years later he applied a similar approach to politics, when he founded the Christian Socialist movement. To him, socialism meant drawing the various classes and parties together into a single brotherhood, welding their ideas and traditions into a common vision of society.

During the twentieth century, ecumenism has played its part in creating great bureaucracies and, at every level of church life, it has woven its own web of committees and officials. But it has also, to a quite remarkable extent, achieved what Maurice wanted: it has opened people's eyes to aspects of truth and of spiritual experience which other Christian denominations possess. And in the process,

Christian worship has been enormously enriched as each denomination has adopted prayers and even rituals from the others. Some have also looked beyond Christianity itself towards other faiths, seeking inspiration in their sacred writings and finding common ground between all the great world religions. Yet in an important respect the ecumenical movement had almost wholly failed to fulfil Maurice's hopes: the different denominations have not united. Their bishops and theologians rake the embers of old doctrinal disputes; and although the heat has faded, they still claim to discern vital differences of view. The laity, now as always, are suspicious of their intellectual leaders, and mostly regard these doctrinal differences as purely semantic. But they see little to be gained, and much to be lost, from merging ecclesiastical institutions: thriving church communities would be submerged, revered traditions would be tossed aside, beloved old buildings would be declared redundant. Why, they ask, can we not be unified in love and mutual respect, and yet remain separate as communities?

The second, more recent movement that has profoundly affected Christian life is the growth of charismatic worship and prayer. In spirit and temper this has much in common with the evangelical revival of the eighteenth century, but today it cuts across the denominational boundaries, enjoying as much support in the Catholic church as in the evangelical Protestant churches. Its most marked characteristic has been glossolalia – speaking and singing in tongues – and in the early years of the movement many regarded this as the sole sign of true Christian conversion. But increasingly other spiritual gifts, such as prophecy, teaching and even administration, have been nurtured in the conviction that every Christian has a distinct and vital ministry. Originally the charismatic movement affected only small groups, and often caused divisions in the local church between those who had 'received the Spirit' and the rest. But now, as the movement grows to maturity, it is permeating the entire church, encouraging lay people to recognise and develop

89

their gifts of ministry, and bringing greater joy and spontaneity to parish worship.

Paradoxically, the charismatic movement is often hostile to ecumenism, and the enthusiasts for church unity are contemptuously dismissed as 'ecumaniacs'. This rises partly from an impatience with the slow pace of ecumenical progress. Church unity, they believe, condemns Christians to laborious negotiations over church buildings, eccleciastical structures, and archaic points of doctrine. But it is also due to a fear that ecumenism will dilute the very essence of Christian commitment. Ecumenics are often liberal and tolerant in their outlook, open to ideas from secular philosophy and from other religions. Charismatics, by contrast, are usually so exited by their love of Jesus, and their lives are so transformed by their relationship with him, that they believe only faith in him can bring salvation.

Yet, despite the antipathy between the ecumenical and charismatic movements, there is a third movement which in many respects embraces both. It is the growth of Christian community life. Since the 1960s numerous communities have sprung up throughout the Western world, in which families and single people have sought to live in closer fellowship than is possible in the normal parish church. Some are formed for a particular purpose, such as caring for the mentally handicapped, or running a conference centre, but many just exist simply for the love and mutual support their members can give to one another, and the daily worship they can share. At present, the movement is in its early stages, and is marked by numerous heroic failures, when high aspirations are frustrated by lack of cash or inefficient management. Yet in the process valuable lessons are being learnt and a stable pattern of community life is emerging.

The typical modern community is both ecumenical in its vision and charismatic in its ministry. Within the context of close personal relationships and daily worship together, the barriers between different Christian traditions quickly break down. Equally, as people become aware of each other's spiritual gifts through daily contact, they naturally want to use them more fully. A hierarchical leadership, in which all the spiritual gifts are focused on a few at the top, is seen as a sinful waste of the talents which God has given to the whole community, and so a charismatic ministry in which every member plays a part is regarded as both sensible and essential. And, if the community is to survive and flourish, then a gentle tolerance must permeate its life, in which variations in religious belief and moral outlook are welcomed as stimuli to deeper insight and understanding. Thus the hostility which charismatics have towards 'ecumaniacs' melts away, and these two movements of the Spirit can progress towards spiritual unity and towards shared ministry, now seen as complementary.

To the outside observer, the Christian scene in the late twentieth century is at best confused, and at worst a noisy drama of petty domestic squabbles. The bitter controversy over the ordination of women masks an even deeper division over the nature of ministry itself, between those who wish to preserve a strict hierarchy, and others who yearn for the old order to crumble, to be replaced by a new charismatic pattern. The bitter controversy between conservatives and radicals over various matters of doctrine masks an even deeper division over the nature of Christian faith between those who regard the Scriptures and creeds as inerrant statements of truth, and those who see faith as an exploration, which can make use of any map or guide, including the literature of other religions. Some may hail the community movement as a sign of the way forward. But others can justly point to the large number of failed communities, compared with the pitiful few who have found some degree of stability. And besides, people may add, community life can only be the vocation of a small minority of Christians, while the majority will always have to live and work in ordinary parishes.

Yet at heart, all Christians are called to some form of community. The books which comprise the New Testament did not emerge out of a vacuum, but are the products of Christians striving together to express their faith. And Christian ministry cannot function in isolation, but exists to deepen and enhance our mutual commitment. Hence, our vision of church and ministry for the future must stem from our theology of community.

The Charismatic Church

Where a group of people come together to form a new Christian community, they have a rare opportunity — to create from nothing, a church. Members of existing denominations must always operate within the institutions and traditions they have inherited, so that new ideas will inevitably get pressed into old moulds before they are put into practice. But those who strike out on their own, to start something entirely fresh, can scrutinise every tradition and question every prejudice to create the pattern of life and ministry which they believe to be right.

This was the challenge which confronted the first monks who trekked out into the deserts of Egypt and Syria in the fourth century. Reacting against the growing wealth and power of the Church, they wanted to return to a primitive simplicity in which their whole lives could be devoted to Christ. The earliest monks lived as hermits in remote caves, but gradually they began to form into small groups to worship together and to support one another in their spiritual battles. It was a former soldier, Pachomius, who organised the original monasteries, in which the monks lived in a self-sufficient village, following a common rule of life. The individual monk continued to enjoy a high degree of independence, living in his own hut, formulating his own discipline and private prayer, and eating most of his meals alone. The community met together once each day for common worship, and on Sundays and festivals for a common meal. They also worked together in the fields and at various crafts, such as weaving and papermaking. The most striking feature, however, was the strict division of leadership, between those with pastoral care of the monks, and those who managed the community's daily life. The pastors were usually older men chosen unanimously by the community for their wisdom and discernment, and their task was to guide the monks in their spiritual progress, to resolve disputes and to maintain discipline. Those who managed the community, by contrast, were younger men, chosen for their energy and intelligence: these included the abbot, with overall responsibility, plus a number of other officers in charge of each activity, such as agriculture, building craft workshops and so on. The pastors commended people to serve in these various positions, who in turn were recognised by the whole community.

The Pachomian pattern reflected closely that of the Jerusalem church, described in the early chapters of Acts, where the apostles were concerned with spiritual matters and evangelism, while seven deacons were appointed to look after the material affairs. And the Pachomain structure stood the test of time: to this day there are monasteries in Ethiopia, organised in precisely the same way as the nine communities which Pachomius founded sixteen centuries ago. In the Western church, however, a quite different style of monasticism developed. By the early seventh century most Western monasteries had adopted the Rule of St Benedict; and, though this contained much gentle wisdom, and even quiet humour, the life it described was far stricter and more hierarchical than that of Pachomius. The monks slept in dormitories, ate all their meals together, and worshipped together many times each day. And all authority, both spiritual and material, resided in the abbot. He decided what work each monk should do, he punished those who misbehaved, and appointed officers to run each aspect of the monastery's life. Thus between Pachomius and Benedict we have two contrasting models of community: in one the individual has a high degree of independence, and authority is dispersed; in the other people live very closely together, and authority is centralised.

Today, the new communities face exactly the same questions as confronted Pachomius and Benedict: how communal should they be? How should decisions be made? Surprisingly, the great majority have found themselves copying Benedict. This is partly because Benedictine tradition has been so dominant in the West for so long, and has influenced so many other institutions such as public schools and theological colleges, that lay people forming a community unconsciously adopt many of its patterns. Thus, typically, the families and single people will pool their income, live in a large house and eat all their meals together, and even attempt to pray together three of four times daily. Decision-making also will be centralised – although, instead of one person's holding authority, the whole group will meet, discussing and voting on each issue as it arises. Yet, while such a model is suitable for a group of single men or women, it soon breaks down under the pressure of family life. Mothers resent having to ask the community for the food and clothes their children need, and yearn for the freedom to buy what they want. The natural instinct to work hard in order to provide for one's family is diluted when the rewards for individual effort are enjoyed fully by everyone. Democratic meetings prove no less oppressive than a rigid hierarchy, because those who are most articulate or most adept at politicking dominate the rest. As a result, communities run on such lines tend to collapse after a few short years, amidst bitter acrimony and lost fortunes.

Gradually, however, the community movement is moving towards a Pachomian model. Just as the Pachomian monks had their own huts, so communities are realising that each family must have its own home, where it sleeps, eats, and relaxes together. And the family must enjoy a high degree of independence, deciding to a great extent how it spends its income and uses its time. Thus the spheres of life in which the community as a whole must make decisions are much more limited – making powerful or interminable meetings unnecessary. This means that authority within the community, both spiritual and material, can readily be dispersed amongst its members so that each person can develop his own gifts of leadership. Such communities thus combine a high degree of stability with a truly charismatic style of ministry.

What lessons, then, does the community movement have for the wider church? What new vision is emerging which can revitalise Christian ministry? The Pachomian separation of pastorship from management is built into the traditional structure of many denominations. In any Anglican parish, for example, there are priest and church-wardens; in a Methodist church there is the minister and the stewards; and amongst Baptists there are often a minister and deacons. Yet the basic ministries have been overlain with a suffocating blanket of committees and councils, condemning active Christians to a ceaseless round of business meetings. The first and most urgent task is to clear away the bureaucracy of the church, to uncover the historic ministries, and allow them to breathe again.

From this follows the second, equally vital task – to look afresh at the role of pastor and manager, minister and deacon, priest and warden. For centuries priests and ministers have been regarded as Benedictine abbots, monopolising the spiritual gifts, and also directing the material affairs of their churches. Small wonder that the history of Christian ministry is largely a depressing account of failure, since few men are capable of fulfilling such a task. The primary purpose of the ordained minister is to perceive, release and encourage the multifarious gifts of his congregation. His own particular spiritual gift must be that of the discernment, enabling him to see the latent talents of others; and he must also have the moral gift of humility, enabling him to rejoice in seeing other people grow into positions of leadership. Amongst the gifts which he must seek in others is that of administration, and he must then commend people to act as 'deacons', managing the church's affairs. The ordained minister himself (or herself) need have no such gifts, and should generally be free of all the administrative burdens which currently fall on the shoulders of the priest and minister.

The practical implications of such a model of ministry are huge. For centuries the ordained minister alone has received an income so that he could work full-time; and he alone has received formal training. As a consequence it is hardly surprising that he has been elevated the status of Benedictine abbot. Instead, it may sometimes be appropriate to set aside people with other gifts to work full-time: evangelists, healers, counsellors and administrators. In a particular area, covering a number of churches, there may be only one full-time pastor and a number of other pastors with secular jobs. In addition, there may be an administrator and even an evangelist and a teacher, who are receiving stipends from the church. Some denominations have attempted to move in this direction by encouraging some clergy to specialise in particular types of ministry, but in practice this has done little to break down the dominance of a clerical elite. Instead, the churches must realise, fully and openly, the different ministries that are needed, and then train and ordain people accordingly. Only then can a truly charismatic style of ministry, in which every gift is used and developed, begin to flourish.

The Pachomian monastery was independent, running its own affairs and appointing its own leaders. But monks from different monasteries often came together to discuss matters of common interest, and an individual monk was free to move from one community to another. Thus each monastery developed its own style and traditions, yet was linked through friendship and prayer to others. If the church today seeks to become charismatic and more communal, then a loose federation between churches and denominations will prove far more beneficial than any kind of giant institution.

Model for Ministry

Too often the ecumenical movement has confused unity with hierarchy: it has sought to bring the bishops and clergy of different denominations into a single structure, with local congregations being compelled to sacrifice their own traditions in order to merge with others. Mercifully, such schemes for merger have usually failed, with the lay people in the pew stubbornly asserting that they can enjoy warm friendship with other churches, and yet retain their own independence. The different denominations and sects, with their various traditions and style of worship, reflect genuine differences in individual needs, so each person should feel free to choose the Christian group that most suits their spiritual temperament.

To the doctrinal purist this raises the question which has so often divided people into warring religious camps – what constitutes true Christianity, and hence which denominations can truly call themselves Christian? It is remarkable how many denominations claim that they alone possess unalloyed truth. In the final two chapters we shall look more closely at the nature of faith itself, and suggest that any such special claims are misplaced. As the Persian mystic, Rumi, said, 'Human language, when applied to divine truth, is a handful of dust, which one breath of God scatters.' Thus, there is no need to draw a thick black circle asserting that those within it are Christian and those without are not. Ecumenism should embrace all who sincerely seek the truth, each individual and each group being open to learn from the insights of others.

Donatus and Pachomius were almost exact contemporaries, but in different parts of North Africa. They and the movements they inspired are rarely linked, since one was condemned as heretical and the other upheld as orthodox. Yet the spirit which prompted them, and the vision of church life and ministry which they sought to put into practice, are remarkably similar. Both reacted passionately against the power-mongering and money-grubbing which infected the bishops and clergy in the late Roman Empire, and both sought to return to the primitive simplicity of the apostolic church. Both believed that Christians must live in close fellowship, supporting one another both spiritually and materially; and both, in different ways, believed that Christian ministry must be charismatic, with every member offering their special gifts for the common good. Both also found themselves in the desert, on the edge of civilisation, Pachomius by choice, and Donatus by force of circumstance. The difference lay in where they applied their vision: Pachomius set up new communities for monks or nuns, while Donatus wanted to transform the parish churches of ordinary towns and villages. Today the community movement must again have this dual application. We need special communities where families and single people pray and work together as Pachomius's monks did, and thus embody, in every aspect of their daily life, the Gospel of Christ. Such communities could then inspire and encourage the ordinary parish churches, where people are inevitably scattered within large neighbourhoods and work in secular jobs, to deepen their fellowship and fulfil their common ministry.

Part 4
Origen

Jesus the Mystic

The Way of Knowledge

Of all the ancient philosophers whose thoughts influenced Christianity in its early centuries, the most important undoubtedly was Plato. He lived in Athens in the fourth century before Christ, and his early ambitions were political. But after the cynical condemnation of the philosopher Socrates, whom Plato had known since boyhood, he concluded that there was no place for a man of conscience in politics. In 387 BC, he founded an academy for the systematic pursuit of philosophical and scientific research, and for the rest of his long life presided over its distinguished activities.

He wrote prolifically, covering almost every field of human endeavour; but throughout his work, even when he was concerned with such matters as law and politics, there was a constant thread of religious mysticism. He believed that originally man's soul contemplated the eternal truths – the Forms or Ideas, as he called them – but that birth into a material body plunged man into a world of illusion and shadows; his ultimate purpose, therefore, is to regain true knowledge. He compared the soul's lot on earth to that of a man trapped in a deep cave, unable to move his head. He can watch, on the wall of the cave, shadows of other people moving, but he can see neither the people themselves nor the source of light at the mouth of the cave. The soul's task is to break free from its imprisonment, to look at the people and things as they truly are, and, finally, by climbing up to the mouth of the cave, to discover the source of all light and life.

The first step, then, of the soul's progress towards truth is to realise that the world of the senses is illusory: that, as we look at the objects and people around, we are not perceiving them as they really are, but merely material shadows of their true selves. Next comes the process of moral purification, which is equivalent to the man in the cave breaking free and turning to the source of the shadows. The soul must detach itself from passions and desires, such as anger and lust, which imprison it within the material realm, and in doing so it will acquire wisdom and tranquillity. Interestingly, Plato gives a high place to music and poetry as aids to detachment, with their rhythms and harmonies sinking deep into the soul and bringing peace. Finally, there is the contemplation of ultimate truth. Contemplation is not simply intellectual knowledge, but rather spiritual unity with the truth: the soul which has climbed out of the cave is wholly immersed in the beauty and warmth of the sun.

At first sight, the refined, other-worldly philosophy of Plato seems wholly at odds with the rugged materialism of the Hebrew culture from which Jesus emerged. And as Christianity encountered Greek thought there was inevitably tension. Some, like Tertullian, believed they could not be reconciled, and that Christianity must wholly reject the pagan philosophers as agents of Satan. But most Greek and Roman Christians sought links between their new faith and the old ideas. This led in the second century to the most widespread heresy, Gnosticism – the 'way of knowledge' – which has ever gripped the church. Gnostics, like Plato, saw the souls as imprisoned within the body, and believed that only through a direct knowledge of God could the soul break free. The various Gnostic sects differed greatly as to how such knowledge was achieved, some professing ideas close to those of Plato, others developing complex cosmologies to describe the spiritual realm.

The main centre of Gnostic thought was Alexandria where, from about the year AD 125, Basilides attracted numerous pupils. He set out to fuse Christian and pagan ideas into a comprehensive philosophy, and this engendered a profound hostility towards the religion of the Old Testament. Basilides' God was remote and mysterious, beyond normal human comprehension, and could be encountered only through long spiritual training. The Yahweh portrayed in the Old Testament was not God at all, but God's enemy, encouraging anger and jealousy amongst men, and so enslaving their souls. Thus God sent his 'Thought' into the world, in the appearance of a human being, Jesus Christ, delivering souls from Yahweh. This liberation consists in becoming detached from the material world by freeing the soul from all emotion and desire, and, as such, detachment is achieved, the soul is fused with God's 'Thought'.

Faced with the testimony of Scripture, Basilides and his followers were extremely selective. For them Christ was a purely spiritual being in total unity with God, so that many of his sayings and the events of his life had to be interpreted allegorically. They were happy with much of St John's gospel where Christ speaks of the unity of his will with that of God. But the practical morality of the other gospels seemed irrelevant, as did the miracles of physical healing, since in Gnostic eyes the material body was an object of contempt. Worst of all, however, was the crucifixion which in the Gnostic view could not have occurred since God cannot suffer; so Basilides concluded that Simon of Cyrene took the appearance of Christ and was crucified in his place.

At this early stage in the history of the Church there was no universal Christian institution, but rather numerous local churches with their own ways of worship, and their own sets of sacred writings. Thus the Gnostics did not form a rival church, but rather in many areas the local church had Gnostic tendencies. Usually a Gnostic church would have an elite of 'pneumatikoi' – spiritual beings – who had received enlightenment; then there would be an outer group of 'psychikoi', who were being trained. Most Gnostics were highly ascetic, mortifying the flesh in all sorts of imaginative ways to help free the soul. Some showed their contempt for the body by going to the other extreme, indulging in sexual and drunken orgies.

The most influential Gnostic leader, whose teaching still raises acute questions for us today, was a wealthy shipowner called Marcion. Like Basilides, he made a radical distinction between Yahweh, as described in the Old Testament, and God revealed in Christ. Yahweh was the creator of the material world, and ruled it by a system of punishments and rewards, embodied in the Jewish law. The God of Christ, by contrast, created human spirits which he ruled through grace. The conflict between law and grace, described by Paul in his epistles, is thus at heart the battle between the material and the spiritual realms; and, through Christ, the spiritual realm can be victorious. Marcion was a great scholar, and was the first to make a detailed study of all the sacred Christian writings in circulation, in order to form a canon of Scripture. He concluded that the true Christian revelation is contained in the main epistles of Paul, cutting out all references to Abraham and other Hebrew figures, and, in the middle section of Luke's gospel, excluding both the Nativity and the Resurrection accounts, since they were too materialistic in their portrayal of Jesus.

Marcion was a tireless evangelist, making converts and founding churches throughout the Roman world. Like all Gnostic churches, they were hierarchical, with a spiritual elite who ruled the rest; and the elite's way of life was monastic in its rigour, with sexual relations and material pleasures strictly forbidden. Although many pagans were attracted to Marcion's gospel, most people who were already Christian resented the extra demands he was making, and were incensed also by his severe pruning of the sacred Christian books. At their height, Marcion's groups could in many areas rival the older churches in strength, but after Marcion's death in 160 they diminished rapidly, and took permanent root only in parts of Syria.

Gnostic Christianity, as taught by Basilides and Marcion, was too exclusive and too ascetic ever to have enjoyed popular support. Moreover, its contempt for material creation is at odds not only with the Old Testament, but also with much of the teachings of Christ as handed down by the apostles; hence both Marcion and Basilides were forced to edit and distort even those books of which they approved. Yet Gnosticism raised questions and contained insights which are fundamental. Christians today continue to find the Yahweh, as described in much of the Old Testament, difficult to reconcile with the God of whom Christ preached. Often Yahweh seems cruel and vengeful and, at times, even ignorant and crass, while Christ's God is loving, merciful and omniscient. More importantly, the Gnostics stressed that direct contemplation of God is possible for all who sincerely seek it: the Christian faith is not a matter of intellectual belief, in which the individual assents to a series of doctrines, but a spiritual experience in which the Christian gradually comes to know God for himself. Though Gnostism as such had virtually died out by the end of the second century, the mystical yearning which it expressed can never be crushed – and in the third century it re-emerged again in Alexandria, with even greater force.

The Mystical Eunuch

In the latter part of the second century, the Bishop of Alexandria, Demetrius, ran a school for pagans who wished to learn about Christianity. Its purpose was to present the Christian faith as the fulfilment of the ancient philosophies, so the bishop employed teachers who were adept at intellectual debate and also well-versed in classical literature. For twenty years the principal of the school was the benign and erudite Clement. In Clement's view the Greek philosophy of Plato, no less than the Hebrew ideas of the Old Testament, had prepared mankind for receiving the full truth in Christ. Thus he sought to convince his pagan pupils that the works of Plato pointed the way to the Christian Scriptures.

Clement, in attitude if not in name, was a Gnostic. He wanted the Church to contain a spiritual and intellectual elite, who were both highly educated in Christian and pagan literature, and also spiritually pure and hence free of all base passions. To him, faith in Christ was not the end of the spiritual journey, but a stepping stone on the path to direct knowledge of God. In one respect, however, he differed from the Gnostics: to Clement the material world was not evil but good, created by God as a temporary home for souls. Thus Clement's spiritual elite could be married, eat good food and drink wine, and enjoy all the other natural pleasures of life; the body that is comfortable and happy, according to Clement, will encourage the soul within it to be loving and thankful towards God.

In the year 202, however, Clement's own happiness was destroyed by a sudden and savage persecution of Christians in Alexandria; and, rather than face imprisonment, Clement fled. Bishop Demetrius went into hiding and ruled his diocese through clandestine contacts, and he appointed as the new principal of his school an unknown young man, Origen, then only eighteen years old. Origen's parents had become Christian when he was a child, and during the persecution his father was arrested. Origen, who in his youth was fanatical in his Christian zeal, decided to go to prison and urge his father to embrace martyrdom. It was only his mother's ruse in hiding all his clothes that held him back. When he became principal of the school, Origen was anxious that he would have to teach female pupils, and hence risk being overcome by sexual passion, so he decided to take literally Christ's command to 'become a eunuch for the Kingdom of God' and castrated himself. In contrast to Clement's comfortable existence, Origen ate only a few raw vegetables and beans, and allowed himself the minimum of sleep, so that he could pursue his scholarly endeavours through the night. He refused any payment from Demetrius for his work, and instead sold his father's library of classical literature, and used the proceeds to provide for his meagre needs.

Although he prayed for martyrdom, and although a number of his closest friends were executed in the persecution, Origen himself was never touched by the authorities. As the persecution eased, Origen began to mix widely, not only with fellow Christians, but also with pagans, even attending lecture courses in Platonic philosophy. Like Clement, he believed that Plato's ideas were God-given tools with which to penetrate the mysteries of Christ; and if Christians and pagans alike could be persuaded of this, then pagans would become Christian, and Christianity would be greatly enriched. This led Origen towards the task that was to absorb his energies for almost half a century – interpreting the Scriptures in the light of Greek philosophy. He accepted Marcion's view that taken literally the Old Testament presented a monstrous portrayal of God, and he scoffed at those who read the Genesis story as historical fact. 'Who is so silly,' he asked, 'to think that God like some farmer planted a paradise eastwards of Eden?' But, rather than reject the Hebrew scriptures, Origen sought to interpret them allegorically in order to find a hidden meaning; and the mystical theology he derived from this method profoundly influenced the growth of Christian monasticism in the following century, and in later periods affected Christian figures as diverse as Meister Eckhart and John of the Cross, Jacob Boehme and Nikolai Berdyaev.

For Origen, the pivotal books of Scripture are those ascribed to Solomon, Proverbs, Ecclesiastes and the Song of Songs, since these correspond to the three stages of spiritual development. The first stage is virtue. The Book of Proverbs shows how a man 'should amend his behaviour and keep God's commandments'. This will not of itself bring any enlightenment, but provides the necessary exterior condition for inner progress to begin. The second stage is detachment. The philosopher in Ecclesiastes demonstrates 'how empty is the world and how brittle is wealth and fame', so that the 'wise man renounces the world and all that is in it.' The third stage is contemplation, in which the individual desires only 'the things that are unseen and eternal'. To Origen, the Song of Songs is an elaborate metaphor of the soul's relationship to God, in which the passionate mutual attraction between the bride and bridegroom symbolises the unity between the human soul and its divine creator. Thus the bride who 'sits at midday' waiting for her lover is the soul who 'puts himself at leisure in order to see God'. When the bridegroom is 'behind the wall, looking out through the windows, becoming visible through nets', it is Jesus appearing in the 'nets of human flesh' to look face to face at mankind; and when the Song refers to 'the shadow of the apple tree', the shadow is the protection from the heats of worldly passion which faith in Christ provides.

This spiritual progress begins and ends joyfully, but in the middle there are times of hardship when faith and courage are severely tested. In a remarkable passage, Origen uses the entire Old Testament story as an allegory of spiritual joy and suffering. The escape from Egypt through the Red Sea stands for the conversion and baptism of the Christian, which brings a great sense of inner freedom and lightness of spirit; in this early period the soul is full of hope, and prayers are readily answered by God. Then comes a long period of dry journeying through the desert, and bloody battles fought against enemy tribes: these stand for spiritual dryness and for constant struggle against bodily temptations which the soul must withstand. Yet whenever Israel is near to despair and defeat, God raises up a prophet to give guidance and encouragement; likewise God will never test the individual soul beyond its endurance, but teach the soul through suffering how to love and trust more fully. The coming of Christ, foretold by the prophets, is the final reward of Israel's faithfulness – and is the light that can fill every soul.

While Origen could treat the Bible as an allegory, his theology could remain firmly on the spiritual plane, and so be wholly agreeable to minds steeped in the philosophy of Plato. But there were two hard material facts contained in Scripture that Origen could not escape: that the universe was created by God; and that Jesus was a human being, made of flesh and blood. Thus Origen developed his own idiosyncratic cosmology. Originally God created angels that were 'wholly pure', but at some moment these angels had become bored and rebellious, and so were cast out of heaven to live at a great distance. God then created the world to be a material home for these fallen angels, and as souls they now inhabit bodies. This is not a punishment, but rather an opportunity to learn afresh how to be united to God. The ultimate purpose of the soul, therefore, is to be restored to heaven by severing its material attachments, and ascending to God through prayer and contemplation.

The doctrine of incarnation had always presented a particular problem to Christians imbued with the ideas of Plato. For Origen, the divine Logos is 'the breath and power of God', who is the 'highest of angels'. When the angels fell, the Logos remained pure, and became the agent of God in creating the material world. In Christ, the Logos took flesh, so that as we encounter Christ we are indirectly seeing God. But this is only the preliminary stage: the goal of Christian life is for the individual soul to 'see behind the flesh' of Christ, and contemplate directly the divine Logos.

Origen himself was austere in the extreme, making his predecessor Clement seem like a hedonist by comparison. Yet, like Clement, Origen wanted to affirm the material world as having positive spiritual value, recognising it as God's creation. In some of his more obscure passages, he seems to be saying that the material realm offers a mirror of the spiritual realm. In particular, the five material senses reflect five 'spiritual senses'. Thus, when in John's gospel Christ speaks of himself as the 'bread of life', he is referring to a spiritual sense of taste; and when he calls himself the 'light of the world', he is speaking of spiritual sight. As the soul contemplates God, these spiritual senses are dramatically heightened, giving intense spiritual joy.

Throughout his writings, Origen was in constant danger of falling between two stools, the Christian and the Platonist. His theory of spiritual senses was abhorrent to a true Platonist whose image of the soul was much too abstract and rarefied to allow any such possibility. And his strange cosmology, giving only a subordinate place to the Incarnation, and giving no place at all to the Holy Spirit, was to many less speculative Christians a grave affront.

Canons and Creeds

Marcion, the famous Gnostic, saw Paul as expressing the essence of Christianity. This was partly because Paul's sharp contrast between the law and the Gospel allowed Marcion to cast aside the entire Old Testament. But more fundamentally it was because, in Marcion's eyes, Paul stressed direct religious experience, as distinct from the mere acceptance of doctrine. Marcion, like other Gnostics, was not interested in objective facts, so that any debate about whether the Crucifixion and Resurrection actually occurred, at a particular place and time, was irrelevant. And Maricon saw in Paul an ally. When Paul speaks of the Resurrection, he almost invariably relates it to the personal experience of 'dying with Christ', with one's 'sins nailed to the cross'. Even more strikingly, the resurrection for Paul was first and foremost his own vision of the resurrected Christ on the road to Damascus, and he subsequently wrote of how every Christian can 'rise to new life'.

Yet paradoxically, by making his own collection of sacred texts, Marcion gave a sharp impetus to the quest for orthodoxy. Gnosticism could flourish while every local church had its own compendium of sacred texts, allowing the spiritual elite of that church to add their own writings to the local bible. So in the second century all manner of gospels and epistles were circulating, many, like the gospel of Thomas, containing the most fanciful ideas and speculations. Marcion, though as a Gnostic he should have rejoiced at such freedom, yearned for strict order in which his version of Gnosticism would prevail. Thus his opponents were compelled to beat him at his own game. They used two weapons. The first was to draw up a 'rule of faith' – a creed – to state explicitly the central tenets of Christianity as handed down from the apostles. The second was to decide which books were written by an apostle – or someone closely associated with an apostle – and declare that those books alone should be read publicly at worship.

The main champion of orthodoxy was Irenaeus, bishop of Lyons in Gaul in the late second century. His five books, entitled *Against the Heresies*, were masterly refutations of both the New Prophecy of Montanus and of the various Gnostic sects. Against Marcion and the Gnostic the crucial issue was authority. According to Irenaeus, the worldwide Church had 'received from the apostles and their disciples its faith', which could be summarised in three statements: that there is 'one God the Father Almighty, maker of heaven and earth; there is one Christ Jesus the Son of God who was made flesh for our salvation; and there is one Holy Spirit who through the prophets proclaimed the virgin birth, the passion, the Resurrection, and the bodily ascension into heaven of our beloved Lord Jesus Christ.' In one form or another this trinitarian structure was applied to all subsequent creeds. But Irenaeus's creed had an extra element, later diluted or dropped, that the entire story of Christ was predicted in the Old Testament. Iranaeus had thus firmly asserted that the Hebrew scriptures should form the first part of the Christian Bible.

Agreeing on the second part, however, was more complex, since it was far from clear which books in current circulation had apostolic authorship. The first three gospels all enjoyed widespread support outside Gnostic circles, as did the epistles of Paul. The Eastern and Western churches were at loggerheads over the Epistle to the Hebrews, since the former believed it was by Paul, while the latter were certain it was of later authorship. Only in the fourth century did the Western churches include it as authentic – a decision which modern scholarship refutes! It was the gospel of John, however, which proved most awkward. Many Gnostic sects (though not Marcion) regarded it as the most important single text, and various Gnostic commentaries on it were widely read. So, if for no other reason, this made the proponants of orthodoxy suspicious of it. But Irenaeus skilfully argued that both it and the Book of Revelation were by the apostle John, and on this basis it was finally included – another decision whose basis is widely doubted by modern scholars, who generally regard the evangelist as different from the apostle.

By the time of Origen the issues were largely settled, and Origen regarded himself as a staunch defender of orthodoxy. And, from about 210, he became a world celebrity, being invited to lecture to churches all over the Christian world, and to resolve doctrinal disputes. On one occasion, the Empress herself, who was sympathetic to Christianity, summoned him to give 'a sample of his universally admired insight into divine things'. But as his reputation grew, so did opposition to him, and many came to regard his as a Gnostic in new guise. Again the central issue was authority. Origen believed that as a theologian he should be free to pursue whatever lines of thought he deemed important, and to publish his ideas and speculations for all to read; it was then for others to test and criticise these ideas in the light of their own faith. Bishop Demetrius, who had first appointed Origen, regarded such freedom as dangerous, threatening the authority of the bishops and clergy to determine which doctrines should be taught; and many, spurred by jealously of Origen's fame, urged Demetrius to curb him.

Origen's solution was eminently simple: that Demetrius should ordain him priest, so that he could combine his freedom as a theologian with the official authority of the Church. To Demetrius such a move would only worsen matters, since it would sanction Origen's wild speculations. The issue was brought to a head when Origen was lecturing in Caesarea, where the local bishop was a former pupil. Origen, apparently on a sudden impulse, asked the bishop to ordain him, which he duly did. On his return to Alexandria he found Demetrius was furious, and in 231 a synod of Alexandrian clergy banished Origen, and declared his priesthood void on the grounds that he was a eunuch! Origen settled in Caesarea where he continued to write and teach for a further twenty years. During the persecution under Emperor Decius in 252, Origen was arrested and tortured on the rack, but to his annoyance he was denied martyrdom, and died of old age two years later.

But Origen's banishment and death did not end the controversy over his teaching. On the contrary, it grew more acute, continuing at least for three further centuries until he was formerly condemned at the Fifth Ecumenical Council in 553. And, in varying forms, Origenist ideas have been disputed ever since – even as recently as 1928 when an attempt to include him in the Anglican Calendar of Saints raised a storm of orthodox protest. The explicit reasons for his condemnation are that the Son of God is, in Origen's scheme, subordinate to the Father; and that for Origen the Resurrection was a purely spiritual event. But beneath this lay a much deeper issue – that Origen's views are, in some vital respects, akin to those of the arch-heretic Arius and, arguably to those of Pelagius and Donatus as well.

Like Arius a century later, Origen saw Christ as, in essence, no different from all other human beings. To Origen, the Logos is like any other human soul, and Christ's flesh at the Incarnation is like the flesh in which every soul on earth is 'wrapped'. The importance of Christ is that, while all other souls have fallen, the Logos alone remains in union with God. Arius was not directly influenced by Origen, and was most uneasy with his Platonist style of thought. But, as far as the person of Christ is concerned, the implications for faith are the same: we can identify wholly with Christ, as a human being like ourselves. Like Pelaguis a century and a half later, Origen made each individual, through prayer and moral virtue, responsible for his own salvation. And like Donatus he wanted the Church to be a spiritual community, in which each person freely uses his gifts for the service of all – as Origen himself so conspicuously did.

To Origen, the ultimate test of theology was the personal experience of individual Christians: theology is good if it leads the soul towards God, and bad if it leads the soul away from God. This does not mean that faith is purely subjective: since all human souls are similar, created by one God, their experience of God can be analysed objectively. But the written word, whether in the creeds or Scriptures or in works of theology, can only be a guide, and should never be mistaken for truth itself. Truth can only be attained through the direct mystical encounter of the soul with its Maker.

Model for Prayer

Eckhart's Rebirth

When we look back to the medieval Church – and, indeed,
beyond it to the Church of the 'Dark Ages' – we imagine it
to have been a solid and unshakeable monolith. Certainly
there were frequent power struggles at the top, and even, at
one point, two men both claimed to be Pope. But as far as
the ordinary diocese or parish was concerned, it is assumed
that everyone passively accepted the creeds or doctrines
handed down from above, acknowledging without question
the authority of the ecclesiastical hierarchy. A closer look,
however, reveals a much more turbulent, and even anarchic
picture. The hierarchy tried to claim absolute authority, but
in every part of Europe there was all manner of small movements and sects which created their own brands of religion,
often with a strongly mystical flavour. By the late thirteenth
century the hotbed of heresy was Germany, which such
groups as the Brethren of the Free Spirit teaching that
every person is divine and can experience direct union
with God.

It was into this feverish spiritual climate that the greatest
mystic of the medieval period, Meister Eckhart, was born.
His father was the steward of a knight's castle in the
Thuringian Forest, and frequently in later years Eckhart
referred to the human soul as 'a little castle so high above
every road that no man can steal it'. In 1275, at the age of
fifteen, he entered a Dominican friary, and ten years later
was ordained priest. But it was not until he was over forty
that he began to write the booklets and preach the sermons
which made him famous. His first published work was

The Call to Heresy

Talks of Instruction, charmingly subtitled 'Advice offered by Brother Eckhart to such of his spiritual children as asked him about various matters as they sat together after dinner in the evening.' To the modern reader these talks seem pedestrian, with only occasional flashes of brilliance, but they made sufficient impact for Eckhart to be sent to the great university of Paris to teach, and then seven years later to become vicar of Bohoemia, a position of considerable power. It was now, amidst heavy administrative duties which required him to travel extensively, that he wrote his greatest works. At first reading they seem to flow from the pen of someone with nothing else to do but to sit quietly and contemplate God; but their real purpose was to show how God is present and active in the everyday world – and how the busiest of people can become true mystics.

The spiritual path, as Eckhart describes it, has four stages – the first three of which correspond roughly to Origen's stages of spiritual growth. The first starts from the recognition that everything, every tiny insect and every small stone, is an 'expression of God's Word'; and so, in looking at insects and stones, we are seeing reflections of God. God, for his part, 'finds joy and rapture in all things'. Just as a horse, when the tether is taken off, 'pours forth its whole strength in leaping about the meadow', so God 'pours his own strength and whole being into his work of creation, enjoying all his creatures.' Once we perceive this truth, then we will want to act virtuously, caring for all God's creation, not out of a burdensome sense of duty, but because we share God's pleasure in seeing all creatures flourish.

The second stage, which at first seems to contradict the first, involves 'letting go' of the material world by severing our attachments to particular objects and things. Just as creation is the expression of God, so also in relation to God creation is nothing: God does not depend on what he has created, and 'the whole universe, compared to the greatness of God, is as nothing.' To Eckhart, human sin consisted in the individual putting his own ego above God.

Model for Prayer

This may take the form of obvious sins, like greed or lust, but many people, who are outwardly virtuous, inwardly set their own intellects and will-power on the 'highest pedestal', and so are no less sinful than the glutton or fornicator. We are thus called to renounce not only material wealth and power, but also mental power, including even our attempts to understand God by rational thought. As Eckhart put it, in typical paradox, 'the highest and loftiest thing that man can do is to renounce God for the sake of God.' As we let go of ourselves, so we allow 'God to be God', pouring himself into our souls. The process of letting go reaches its climax at the point of stillness: 'nothing in all creation is so like God as stillness, because in stillness God can truly work and speak.' And it is now that the third stage begins, in which, in Eckhart's words, 'the father brings his son to birth within the human soul'. Eckhart found the orthodox doctrine, that Christ's death ransoms souls from the devil, quite repulsive; instead, following Abelard, he saw the Crucifixion as an example – a 'reminder' – of the profound truths that we in our worldly lives forget. Thus, far from being unique, Christ is the model which all of us are invited to emulate. He speaks of the soul as the 'virgin mother' who is impregnated with God's seed; and, as the seed grows, we are 'born again' in the image of God. So, every time a soul 'lets go' and surrenders itself to God, 'the Son of God is born anew'.

The fourth stage is one that is unusual in mystical writers, and does not appear in Origen's works: it is the call of every truly holy person to be a prophet, sharing in Christ's mission to the world. Eckhart is critical of those who make prayer an excuse for ignoring the injustices of the world. On the contrary, he writes, 'even if you are in great spiritual rapture, and you learn of a sick person who needs a bowl of soup, it is far better that you leave your rapture and make the soup.' For the person who has been through the first three stages of spiritual development, love of neighbour will no longer be a moral duty, but a natural pleasure, cheerfully undertaken. Contemplation of God is not, for Eckhart, an end in itself, but a means of becoming a perfect servant of others in the world: 'What we plant in the soul through contemplation, we shall reap in the harvest of action.'

In 1320, at the age of sixty, Eckhart was appointed professor at Cologne. The local archbishop was waging a fierce campaign against the mystical groups that were proliferating there, and he soon concluded that Eckhart's sermons and lectures were 'inciting the ignorant and undisciplined people to wild spiritual excesses'. He accused Eckhart of heresy, and the Inquisition appointed a commission to investigate. It questioned Eckhart closely, and in his defence he compared his own teaching to that of Origen. The commission, however, compared him to the Beghards, a Dutch group who a century earlier had been condemned for the erotic imagery of their mystical teaching. Eckhart was convicted in 1327, and died a year later.

Yet no ecclesiastical commission or court could stem the tide of mystical literature that swept across Europe in the decades after Eckhart. In Britain, for example, Walter Hilton and the anonymous author of 'The Cloud of Unknowing' invited their readers to follow a spiritual journey remarkably similar to that of Eckhart – and indeed to that of Origen. And Richard Rolle and Mother Julian used erotic imagery that can still cause us to blush. Rolle, at one point, uses the sexual act itself as a metaphor for divine contemplation. The mystics attracted huge followings, especially amongst ordinary peasants and tradesman who rejoiced at the spiritual warmth and joy which mystical prayer offered. Most of the mystics, like Eckhart, pleaded their orthodoxy. But, in asserting the freedom of the individual to seek direct communion with God, the mystics were subverting the authority of the medieval Church, which claimed that its doctrines and sacraments alone offered the path to salvation.

Two centuries after Eckhart his native country became

the cradle of the Protestant Reformation. Luther, like Eckhart, preached that the individual could enjoy a direct relationship with God; and like Eckhart, Luther was condemned as a heretic by the Catholic Church. But Luther, and his Swiss counterpart Calvin, had little sympathy with mysticism. For them, God communicated with mankind through words – the words of Scripture – and salvation consisted in understanding and believing the ideas these words contained. Thus, while the Reformers differed from the Catholic Church in the doctrines they taught, Protestants and Catholics alike agreed that the essence of faith is belief: the faithful Christian is one who believes that the doctrines and dogmas of the Church are true.

This emphasis on faith as belief put Catholic and Protestant in the same camp when, from the seventeenth century onwards, Christianity faced the most serious challenge of its entire history: the rise of science. Stone by stone science chipped away at the edifice of orthodoxy, until by the late eighteenth century the very nature of religious belief itself was under threat. Theologians of both the Protestant and Catholic churches proved no match for the scientists or the secular philosophers who provided science with its intellectual tools. Mystical Christianity, by contrast, could watch the rise of science with equanimity; indeed many Christians of mystical inclination welcomed the discoveries of science as affirming their spiritual insights. With their emphasis on direct experience, which transcends human logic, the mystics could offer a religious faith that both embraced the sciences, and also placed scientific discovery in its true perspective.

Science against Religion

In the early seventeenth century the British philosopher Francis Bacon propounded his new scientific method. In the past, he argued, theories about the natural order had been derived through a process of deduction. In particular, theologians had studied the Bible, and from its various stories and statements had worked out the laws of nature. But, said Bacon, the scientist who is sincerely interested in the truth should take the exact opposite approach. He must 'start by making careful observations of the particular workings of nature; and then gradually seek to discern general principles that are consistent with these observations.' This came to be called the 'inductive method'. Bacon mocked the theologians who took every event, whether good or bad, as confirmation of their doctrines. For example, when a man who prays to God is saved from a shipwreck, his escape is ascribed to God's power; but, equally, when a prayerful man is drowned, it is assumed that God wanted to harvest his soul. Bacon urged men to put aside all such 'theological opinions', and embark instead on a journey of scientific enquiry.

As Bacon was stirring controversy in Britain, Galileo was being condemned in Rome for following Bacon's scientific method. He had studied the movements of the sun and the stars across the sky, and concluded after exhaustive calculations that the earth was not the centre of the universe, but moved around the sun – as, indeed, the Polish astronomer Copernicus had suggested a century earlier. Galileo was vilified from pulpits as 'that satanic mathematician', and spent the final eight years of his life under house arrest. The new sciences threatened the Church authorities in the same way that the mystics had done so three centuries earlier. Scientist and mystic alike denied the Church's monopoly of the truth, and asserted their freedom to explore the truth for themselves. Yet, despite his disgrace, history was on Galileo's side. And by the time Newton was seeking to extend Galileo's theories later in the seventeenth century, scientists throughout Europe had broken loose from the Church, and were freely exchanging ideas and information.

Bacon and Newton both had strong religious views,

and devoted as much time to theology as to science. They took it for granted that God had created the universe, and instituted the laws of nature, so ultimately there could be no contradiction between theology and science. Newton saw God as the perfect engineer, who had set the various mechanisms of nature into motion, and then withdrawn from any further involvement. This view came to be known as 'deism', and had profound influence not only on scientific attitudes but also on social and moral ideas. When the economist Adam Smith wrote of the Invisible Hand, which caused the selfish actions of individuals to lead to the greatest prosperity for all, his image of society corresponded precisely to Newton's view of the universe: individuals in the market-place are like stars in the sky, each moving according to its own internal laws to create total harmony.

But in the mid-eighteenth century even deism found itself under attack, its bland optimism torn apart by a new generation of philosophers. The most penetrating blows came from the German writer, Immanuel Kant. He was concerned not with natural laws, but with how we see and understand the world around us, and he called for a 'Copernican revolution' in our ideas about knowledge itself. The human mind, Kant argued, is not a mere passive recipient of information from outside, but imposes its own 'concepts' on what the senses pick up. Even such basic categories as space and time are human concepts, which the mind imposes on the sights and sounds and smells that pour into it. It follows from this that knowledge of God could only be established either if we were directly aware of him, or if he were a category like space and time which is necessary to our understanding of the world. And, according to Kant, God fulfils neither requirement. At best we can only guess at his existence by observing the natural order – and, in Kant's view, the deism of Bacon and Newton was no more than a reasonable guess. Moreover, the ordinary human being can think intelligently about the world without any theological categories. Hence all the traditional proofs of God's existence, and all the finely honed doctrinal formulae of the Church, fall to the ground.

What place, then, is left for religion? Kant himself wanted to reserve a role for faith, and argued that belief in the prospect of rewards and punishments after death was a necessary incentive to make people act morally. Not surprisingly, this contention carried little force, especially since the demolition of all proofs of God's existence implied that the existence of heaven and hell could not be proven either. Few scientists after Newton paid much attention to theology, and when, a century later, Napoleon asked the French astronomer Laplace what place God had in his theory of the cosmos, Laplace witheringly replied 'I have no need for that hypothesis'. In the popular imagination the triumph of science over religion was sealed by Darwin's theory of evolution, when the account of creation in the Book of Genesis was disproved. Although sixteen centuries earlier Origen had dismissed as a fool anyone who took the Genesis story literally, churchmen continued to assert its historical accuracy; and, so Darwin's ideas were widely regarded as the final assault on Christian orthodoxy. By the middle of the nineteenth century many regarded religion as outdated, with no part to play in the modern world.

Yet large numbers of people continued stubbornly to hold on to religious faith and worship, and intelligent men and women continued to turn their minds to questions of theology. In the face of the combined attacks of science and philosophy, two types of religious thought emerged, both of which in different ways answered Kant's criticisms – but which at first sight are fundamentally opposed to one another. The champion of the first was Friedrich Schleiermacher, whose famous *Addresses on Religion, to its Cultured Despisers* appeared at the turn of the eighteenth and nineteenth centuries. Unlike Kant, Schleiermacher believed that man is capable of direct awareness of God, not through intellectual knowledge or moral action, but through 'feeling'. This feeling is 'the consciousness of being absolutely dependent, or, which is the same thing, of being in relation to God.' Dependence on God leads in turn to a sense of the wholeness of creation, that within the manifold diversity of the universe there is unity. Schleiermacher had been educated in Moravian schools, and retained throughout his life a deep and warm Christian piety. But his view of religion led him to conclude that Christian doctrines could have no objective rational truth, but are simply 'accounts of the Christian religious affections set forth in speech'. This does not mean that religion is purely subjective, since consciousness of God must be nutured and shaped within a religious community. Nor does it mean that the Bible has no authority, since the stories and teachings of Scripture are for Christians vital in giving outward expression to inward spiritual affections. But it does imply that Christianity – and indeed every religion – can no longer participate in intellectual, moral or social debate, since religion is at heart a purely private matter, of interest only to those who practise it.

A century later, in the aftermath of the Great War, a quite different approach to Christianity exploded from the pen of Karl Barth. If Schleiermacher responded to Kant's first objection to religion, Barth took issue with the second. Barth asserted that belief in God, and acceptance of divine revelation in Christ, are essential to our understanding of truth. To Barth, God stands 'over against' the natural order, and can never be embraced within human consciousness. Yet in Jesus Christ, God freely chose to reveal himself, and hence challenged mankind to accept or reject his saving grace. Thus faith for Barth consists not in feelings or affections, nor in any kind of subjective experience; on the contrary, faith is a deliberate and decisive 'yes' to the objective truth of Jesus Christ, as the revealed Word of God. This means that Christian theology is a true science, dealing with actual 'data' contained in the New Testament, and should be pursed with the utmost scientific rigour. To this end Barth himself in 1927 embarked on the first volume of *Church Dogmatics*, a project that was still incomplete when he died four decades later. In this great work he intended to submit all the main Christian doctrines to the closest scrutiny, in order to state with the utmost clarity the essence of what God has revealed about himself.

No one can fail to be impressed by the sheer power and majesty of Barth's vision, yet few have been able fully to accept it. At heart Barth is asking us to accept that 'revelation' is, in Kant's sense, a human concept as basic as those of space and time, and that the life of Jesus Christ, as described in the pages of the New Testament, is the only event in history which can be recognised as an authentic revelation. If this were correct, then Christianity could successfully withstand Kant's assaults; but, even for those who would love to share his convictions, Barth's theology is, quite literally, incredible.

Christianity thus seems caught in a trap. In the face of the natural sciences and the secular philosophies, it has been forced to abandon the intellectual high ground, recognising that its doctrines can no longer command the same universal respect as the theories of physics and mathematics. Yet both its lines of escape seem to lead towards blank walls. If it follows Schleiermacher it is reduced to mere pious feelings, albeit sustained by ancient traditions and worshipping communities. Yet if it follows Barth it turns itself into a false science, craving for objectivity when the data from which it works can be seen only through the eyes of faith. Though this trap seems tighter today than ever before in history, it has threatened Christianity since its inception. Origen, in dealing with the pagan philosophies of the ancient world, was familiar with this fundamental dilemma of Christian belief, as were the medieval mystics a millenium later. More strikingly, there is in the writings of the apostle Paul a mystical element which to a remarkable extent anticipates the problems posed by Kant. So it is to Paul and Origen, and to their mystical way, that we must turn for guidance.

Resurrection Living

Paul wrote to the Corinthians: 'If Christ has not been raised, your faith is futile.' Before his own conversion Paul had doubtless heard stories about the Resurrection of Jesus, and had perhaps been struck by how many people claimed to have seen Jesus after his crucifixion. But, even if the unconverted Paul had wondered about the truth of these stories, he would not have been impressed. Miracles of all kinds were being reported daily in first century Palestine; and, as Jesus himself had said, the miracle-workers were more likely to be agents of evil, motivated by greed and pride, than prophets of God.

But then, on the road to Damascus, the risen Christ appeared to Paul himself, and suddenly a bald historical fact became an event pregnant with divine significance. The Resurrection was not merely another miracle, designed to impress the gullible. It was a profound mystery, through which the deepest purposes of God were revealed. Paul's own life was transformed, and he devoted all his energies to seeking to understand this mystery, and to proclaiming it to others. In his Epistles, ideas and insights tumble over one another as he struggles to share the truths he has perceived. Yet through the intellectual and emotional maze of his writings, we can discern three recurring themes in his reflections on Christ's resurrection.

The first is that the Resurrection has changed mankind's moral status from that of slave to that of mature adult. In Paul's eyes the Old Testament law had been created by God to guide men in their ignorance, and so it had to be obeyed blindly, as a slave obeys his master. But now, through the risen Christ, we can have a direct relationship with God, in which we become God's partners in establishing his kingdom on earth. In Jesus Christ we can see the perfection to which God is calling all mankind, and so we can understand the ultimate purpose to which our moral choices should be directed. Hence, in every sphere of human conduct, we are called through Christ's spirit to think for ourselves as to how best God's kingdom can be served. The second theme is that, in the death and Resurrection of Christ, we have the model for all true spiritual experience. Paul speaks time and again of how we are 'buried with Christ . . . our old self crucified with him': we must 'nail' all our sinful attitudes and attachments to the cross of Christ. Only when we have shared Christ's passion, can we be 'united with him in resurrection', and so 'walk with him in the newness of life.' There is no easy, cheap way of attaining spiritual joy; rather, we must undergo a hard, and often painful process of 'dying to sin' in order to 'live for righteousness'.

The third theme is immortality: Christ's resurrection contains the promise of eternal life for all who follow God's way. Traditional Jewish thought had given little attention to life after death, and Greek philosophy generally made a sharp division between body and soul, with only the soul enjoying immortality. Paul was convinced that, in the Resurrection of Christ, God had shown that the whole person, body and soul, would live beyond death. Paul's thoughts on this are often confused, but the point is clear: union with God in Christ does not take us away from the material world into some purely spiritual realm; on the contrary, true holiness finds expression in practical, down-to-earth concern for one's neighbours and for the material injustices of the world.

Albert Schweitzer described Paul's faith as 'mystical'. And, at the risk of imposing artificial order on Paul's thought, we can discern in his three major themes the outlines of the mystical path of Origen, Eckhart and innumerable other spiritual writers. The journey starts with morality, in which the individual takes full responsibility for his outward behaviour. It continues with a long trek through a 'desert' or 'dark night' in which the soul becomes 'detached' from material anxieties and ambitions. And it ends joyfully in the eternal 'light' of God's love. But the journey is not simply linear; it is also circular, as the joyful soul turns back towards the world, to help those in need and to proclaim God's kingdom on earth.

Yet, what authority does Paul have for his 'mystical' teachings? What right does he have to construct such a theology on the foundation of his vision on the Damascus road? And on what basis can Origen, Eckhart and others speak with such conviction about the spiritual path? The question of authority troubled Paul deeply, and it was constantly forced back to his attention as his opponents in Corinth and elsewhere sought to undermine him. Paul acknowledged that his experience was subjective, that on the road to Damascus Christ had appeared to him alone, and that the sense of moral freedom, of dying and rising with Christ, and of receiving God's promise of eternal life, were all personal to himself. Yet, he claimed, these experiences were based on objective, universal truth. Christ's resurrection was not only an individual vision, but also a historical fact, to which a 'cloud of witnesses' could bear testimony. And the spiritual path which he was treading had been laid down – and lit up – by God himself, for all mankind to follow. Thus the subjective and the objective, the personal and the universal, are not in opposition, but are two sides of one truth.

Paul was writing at the beginning of the Christian era; so within Christian circles he had only his own experience, and that of his closest associates, on which to base his mystical theology. By the time Origen and Eckhart were reinterpreting this theology for their own period, it had been authenticated by the experience of countless thousands of Christians who had followed the same path. And when in our own time such diverse Christians as Evelyn Underhill, C.S. Lewis, Baron von Hugel and Harry Williams – to name only a few British spiritual teachers – describe their own journeys in words which echo the passionate epistles of Paul, then his theology carries an authority which no Corinthian opponent could possibly have envisaged. Two millennia ago Paul's ideas were readily dismissed as the subjective fantasies of a religious fanatic; it is the weight of history which anchors his theology firmly within the realm of objective truth.

At bottom, therefore, Barth and Schleiermacher are not enemies, but offer twin pillars of a Christian faith that can continue to stand tall and strong, even amidst the claims of modern science and philosophy. Kant gave two possible criteria for religious truth: that we can know God directly; and that belief in God is a fundamental human concept. Kant dismissed religion as failing to fulfil either criteria – although he later offered a third, highly dubious, moral criterion that could rescue religion. Schleiermacher, however, replies that we can and do know God directly: our sense of the wholeness of things, and our feelings of absolute dependence, are in effect a direct knowledge of divine love. And Barth replies that God is indeed a fundamental human concept, and that the human mind is therefore as open to divine revelation as it is to the world of space and time. Barth saw his theology as opposed to that of Schleiermacher and his kin; and Schleiermacher was extremely suspicious of the kind of thinking which Barth was to exemplify. Yet, far from being incompatible, the two views are complementary: we have a natural, subjective awareness of God; and also God chooses to reveal himself objectively through specific events and people. Such a balance between the subjective and the objective is to be found throughout the Christian tradition. Paul himself speaks of how God's truth is 'written on men's hearts', and that everyone can 'clearly perceive God in the things he has created', and, of course, he writes repeatedly of the 'revelation of God in Jesus Christ'. But the same balance is also found in every major religion. Hindus, Buddists and Muslims all speak of a natural human awareness of God, and also point to particular people and events which in some special way reveal the nature of God.

The word 'mystical' has a doubtful pedigree, and for some Christians today it implies wild spiritual fantasies, or merely an other-worldly indifference to human affairs. But, at a time when so much religious language has become debased, it is the best word at our disposal to describe the balance between the subjective and the objective in religious faith. The great mystics of the Christian tradition, from Origen and the desert fathers, through Eckhart and Mother Julian, to the major teachers on prayer in our own time, have all pointed us to the light of divine awareness already visible within our own souls, and urged us to make an interior journey towards this light. But with equal force they have taught that this journey cannot be made alone, but requires the guidance of Jesus Christ, through whom God has shown us the way. There is nothing in modern science which has in any respect cast doubt on the truth of this 'perennial philosophy', as Aldous Huxley described it. On the contrary, mystical religion and scientific discovery are complementary. The task of the scientist is to penetrate, by human reason, the mysteries of God's creation; the mystical journey takes us, through contemplation, into the mysteries of God himself.

Conclusion:
The Missionary Church

In 1969 I spent a year as a student at Durham University. I was still an atheist, had hair down to my shoulders and smoked hashish. But having spent the previous year travelling round India visiting Hindu gurus, I was convinced that religion held the key to human fulfilment. Thus I was searching for a religious faith to which I could commit my life. At that time Durham had two theological colleges training men for the ordained ministry, one with a strong Anglo-Catholic bias, the other earnestly Evangelical. I made it my business to get to know members of these colleges, in order to learn about Christianity; and to my surprise I found many were pleased to chat late into the night with this dishevelled hippy. Indeed, I gathered that a group in the Evangelical college were regularly praying for my conversion – much to my arrogant amusement.

A year later their prayers were answered: on Christmas Day 1970 I gave my life to Jesus Christ. But these theological students were not the instruments of my conversion; on the contrary, their well-intentioned attempts to convince me of the truth of Christianity actually deterred me, delaying my conversion. In part this was due to the religious jargon they used. Phrases like 'the Son of God', 'salvation from sin', 'sacramental worship', and even 'leap of faith' peppered their conversation. I recognised that religion carried human beings beyond the normal range of experience, so special words would inevitably be needed to refer to the spiritual realm. But for someone like myself, who was brought up in an atheist home, these

Christians seemed at times to be talking a foreign language.

Yet I soon realised that the problem went far deeper than mere language: its roots lay in the ideas – the doctrines – to which those strange phrases referred. Christian faith appeared to me like a large, imposing building, within which everything worked smoothly, but which appeared to have only the most tenuous contact with the outside world. At times, such as when I was taken to a university mission led by David Watson, I was awestruck by the majestic beauty of this edifice: every part of it fitted so perfectly, with no jagged edges or loose stones. And I envied the easy confidence with which Christians scurried round the building, happy in each other's company, and secure within the strong, thick walls. But nothing in the building seemed remotely connected with the ideas and activities of people like me who lived outside its walls. I could hear what they were saying, and even learn the language they were using, but it made no sense, because it did not refer to my own experiences of life.

At the base of this building were two doors. One was marked 'Mission', through which the kind students who spoke to me emerged. But they could only talk to me if I came back into the building with them. They were unable to understand my thoughts and ideas, and could only speak to me within the framework of their own beliefs. And I soon discovered that the main target of their mission was not atheists like me, but lapsed Christians who had learnt the tenets and language of the Christian faith on their mother's knee or at Sunday school. Those who came forward at David Watson's giant gatherings were almost entirely cradle Christians whose faith had been reawakened by his superb oratory.

The second door was marked 'The World', out of which hordes of Christians poured daily to earn their living. Once out in the 'world' they seemed to put aside their Christian faith, and adopt the same patterns of thought and language as the rest of the population – and they were often as shrewd and even as ruthless as atheists and agnostics in acquiring wealth and power, Thus they led double lives, in which Christian and worldly values barely touched.

Twenty years later I am now familiar with this building from the inside. And I have acquired great love and respect for some of the departments within it. In particular I rejoice in its worship, and have learnt that many of the Christian symbols and rituals are profoundly relevant to the needs of the outside world. And the Scriptures, which lie at the base of the building, are as powerful and as fresh as they were 2,000 years ago; indeed, it was when Hindus in India encouraged me to read the New Testament from cover to cover, in order to plumb for myself its spiritual depth, that I fell in love with Jesus. But the department with the word 'Doctrine' on its door remains alien and unfriendly, and its memoranda distorts so much of the good work in the rest of the building. It was the malign influence of this department which prevented the Durham students reaching out to me in my search; and it continues to undermine the entire Christian mission to the majority of our population who, like me, were raised in households indifferent to the Gospel.

To their credit, many Christian theologians have addressed this problem over the past century. And occasionally their books – like *Honest to God* by John Robinson – catch the imagination of the millions of ordinary people who would love to be Christian, but cannot swallow the doctrines. But too often such theologians, in their attempts to make it more acceptable to the modern world, have drained the Christian faith of its passion and vigour. John Robinson himself, like many liberal theologians, was a man of deep piety and devotion, steeped from childhood in the Christian tradition. And when as an atheist I read his great book, it certainly made Christianity seem more plausible. Yet it failed to capture my imagination and my emotions, and I even felt patronised by the author who seemed to be serving me with weak milk, when he himself ate strong meat. Liberal theology could never inspire martyrs!

And so, in my own doctrinal wanderings, I have found myself turning to the major heretics. Far from lacking zeal, they were willing to suffer humiliation, torture and even death for their beliefs. Far from diluting Christianity, they aspired to the highest moral and spiritual ideals. And far from portraying Jesus Christ as a woolly-minded intellectual, their Jesus was a man of passion, on fire with the vision of truth. As one reads the history of Christianity, it is so often the heretics – or those who lean towards heresy – who are most Christ-like, the most generous and the most courageous in their faith. That does not, of course, prove that their teachings are right, since even the most holy men can be in error, but it does demand that they be taken seriously. And amongst the writings of the heretics can be found doctrines which are both plausible and inspiring.

In this book I have explored at length the four great heresies which rocked the early church, and which have continued to stir faithful hearts ever since. I have tried to do justice to the defenders of orthodoxy, and in each case I have concluded that truth lay in some fusion of heresy and orthodoxy. At times the reader may have felt confused at the sheer complexity of the debate. But the conclusions are simple, and together they offer a vision of faith – a creed – which the world today urgently needs, and for which many are desperately hungry. Here is a crude summary of that creed:

1. *Lordship.* Jesus Christ is our Lord and Master, showing the path to perfect love and truth; to be a Christian is simply to follow him on that path.
2. *Prophecy.* Our mission is to open the hearts of people to that love and truth, both by sharing Christ's message, and by changing the political, social and economic institutions in which they live.
3. *Charism.* The Church – the Christian Communion – is

to be a living example of a society based on truth and love, in which all members can use their spiritual and material gifts to the full.

4. *Mysticism*. The ultimate fruit of our faith is for every person to become like Jesus, experiencing for himself the fullness of love and truth; and every aspect of our mission and life together must be tested as to whether it helps individuals towards that goal.

Put in such simple terms, the Christian faith may seem almost banal, compared to the elaborate doctrines which theologians have weaved. And there are many who would regard such a creed as too banal, too simple. They want to be much more precise about the nature of Christ; they want to define how he 'died to save mankind from sin', they want to specify some permanent hierarchical structure for the Church; and, above all, they require that individual freedom in spiritual matters be strictly curbed by doctrinal formulae. The heretics honoured in this book were on the whole very simple in their faith, although at times rather complex in their own self-defence. It is this simplicity which is their attraction to many, but which evokes the suspicion of those in authority.

To be simple in belief is to be strong in faith. The spiritual and practical implications of this heretical creed are huge. A person who does decide to follow Jesus, to share in Christ's prophetic mission, to put his own spiritual and material gifts at the service of the Church, and to strive for the perfect love of God, will find his entire life utterly transformed. There is no room for mental or spiritual wooliness. Being a prophet requires hard intellectual thought, as one seeks to apply the Gospel to modern society. Being a minister means making oneself a channel of divine grace to others. And being a mystic takes one through spiritual deserts and dark nights towards the joy of Christ's risen life. Each of the four major heretics whom I have described saw themselves as fighting complacency and apathy within the Church, and calling Christians back to their primitive faith. It is that same challenge that confronts us today.

For the past century, the Church in the West has been struggling to cope with an intellectual and political climate remarkably similar to that facing it in the second and third centuries. The Church has lost its religious monopoly; it is no longer protected by political rulers, nor do rulers depend on its moral support; and, most important of all, it must preach the Gospel to people who have no prior, childhood knowledge of the faith. There is no need to demolish the great Christian edifice which I first espied in my student days at Durham: so many of its activities are precious, and so much warm love flows along its corridors. But there is an urgent and vital need for a 'Copernican Revolution' in the doctrine department, drastically reducing its size and simplifying its structure.

This in turn will breathe fresh air throughout the rest of the building. Worship will be free from so many of the tired liturgical phrases and wearisome theological sermons which hang over it like a smog cloud. Moral, political and social debate will spring to life, as Christ's Gospel, raw and hard, is applied to the issues of our time. Rigid hierarchies will be shaken loose by a new charismatic spirit, in which every Christian is encouraged to be a minister of Christ. And, most important of all, the Christian mission will engage once again with the real world, seeking to transform the society in which Christians and non-Christians alike must live and work together.

Look at those doors at the base of the building, because it is there that the greatest change must occur. The door marked 'The World' and the door marked 'Mission' must become one huge opening. Those going out into the world, whether as evangelists to convert others, or as workers to earn their livings, are all missionaries with a double task: to share their joy in Christ, and so invite others back; and to change the world itself according to Christ's teaching. The call to heresy, as I have sought to describe it in this book, is at heart the call to each one of us to become Christ's apostles, proclaiming and applying his Gospel to every sphere of human life.

Bibliography

As a recent historian put it, 'we are forced to sing the heretics' ideas to the tunes of their enemies.' The original writings of almost all the great heretics were destroyed as blasphemous, and so we have to reconstruct their ideas from the writings of their opponents. Inevitably this means there is considerable scholarly debate as to what the heretics actually said and meant. In this book I have largely skated over this debate, since my purpose is not primarily to expound the heretics for their own sakes, but to apply their ideas to modern Christianity. I have given as accurate a picture as possible, but any reader wishing to learn more must turn to works of historical scholarship. I commend the following:–

Frend W.H.C., *Saints and Sinners in the Early Church* (DLT London, 1985).

O'Grady Joan, *Heresy* (Element Books, Shaftesbury, 1985).

Wiles Maurice, *The Christian Fathers* (S.C.M., London 1966).

Lough Andrew, The *Origins of the Christian Mystical Tradition* (Clarendon Press, Oxford, 1981).

Von Campenhausen H., *The Fathers of the Greek Church* (A and C Black, London, 1963).

Gregg R. & Groh D., *Early Arianism* (S.C.M., London, 1981).

Williams, R., *Arius* (DLT, London, 1987).

Rees B.R., *Pelagius: A Reluctant Heretic* (Boydell and Brewer, London, 1989).

Frend W.H.C., *The Donatist Church* (OUP, Oxford, 1971).